HELEN EDMUNDSON

Helen Edmundson was born in Liverpool in 1964 and spent her childhood on the Wirral and in Chester. After studying Drama at Manchester University, she gained wide acting, directing and devising experience with the female agit-prop company, Red Stockings. Her first solo writing attempt, *Ladies in the Lift*, a musical comedy, was created specifically for the company in 1988. On leaving, she worked as an actress in various north-west theatres and on television. Her first play, *Flying*, was presented at the Royal National Theatre Studio in 1990.

Her other work includes two short television films: *One Day* (BBC, 1991) and *Stella* (Channel 4, 1992). She has written two acclaimed stage adaptations for Shared Experience Theatre: *Anna Karenina* (1992), which won a Time Out Award and the Theatre Managers' Association Award for Best Touring Production, and *The Mill on the Floss* (1994).

The Clearing (1993) was first performed at the Bush Theatre, London. It was joint winner of the John Whiting Award.

She is married to actor Jonathan Oliver, and lives in West London.

HELEN EDMUNDSON

THE CLEARING

with a historical note by
Peter Berresford Ellis

NICK HERN BOOKS
London

A Nick Hern Book

The Clearing first published in Great Britain in 1994
as a paperback original by Nick Hern Books,
14 Larden Road, London W3 7ST

The Clearing copyright © 1994 by Helen Edmundson

Helen Edmundson has asserted her right to be identified
as author of this Work

Historical Note copyright © 1994 by Peter Berresford Ellis

Typeset by Country Setting, Woodchurch, Kent TN26 3TB
Printed by Cox & Wyman Ltd, Reading, Berks

Front cover: detail from John Derrick's 'Image of Irelande',
published in 1581

A CIP catalogue record for this book is available
from the British Library

ISBN 1 85459 281 5

1000647972

Historical Note
by Peter Berresford Ellis

*The Clearing i*s a play based on grim fact. Ever since the 12th
Century, England had made frequent attempts to conquer and
rule Ireland. *The Clearing* is set against the implementation of
England's most vicious design to solve its 'Irish Question' by
the eradication of the entire Irish nation. It was a genocidal
policy whose resultant folk memories still sit uncomfortably in
the Irish psyche.

By 1652, when this play opens, the Irish nation had been
ruthlessly reconquered by the merciless military machine of
Oliver Cromwell. More than one third of the Irish population,
616,000 men, women and children, had been killed by sword,
plague and famine.

The Irish armies had fought hard to defend their parliament at
Kilkenny but now the last of them had been forced to surrender
and the surviving 40,000 young Irish soldiers and their officers
were forced to transport themselves to Europe to seek service in
the Irish Brigades of such countries as France and Spain.

Within a few more years, the English administration in Ireland
had complacently calculated that its soldiers had arbitrarily
seized and carried off some 100,000 Irish men, women and
children and transported them to the colonies in the Americas,
particularly to Barbados.

With their armies gone, the Irish found themselves without
protection. Some Irish guerrilla bands were formed and fought
back in desperation. They were called Tories, from the Irish
word *toiridhe* – a pursuer. But to no avail. Ireland was flooded
with English soldiers. There is no estimation for the numbers
killed or executed during the years of guerrilla struggle. There
were generally no trials, suspected Tories were killed on
capture. Catholic priests and Presbyterian ministers were
executed whenever they were found. If they were lucky, they
might be shipped off to the colonies.

The descendants of former colonists, who had adopted the Irish language and accepted Irish law and customs were classified as 'mere Irish' by the new English administration and treated in similar manner.

The final enactment of legislative genocide against the Irish took place in the House of Commons on 26 September 1653. An act was passed that was breathtaking in its intent. Before 1 May 1654, all members of the Irish nation were to remove themselves west of the River Shannon into the area of Co. Clare and the province of Connaught, the poorest and most inhospitable region of the island where famine was still raging. If any Irish man, woman or child was found east of the River Shannon after that date they could be immediately executed. The choice was 'Hell or Connaught!'

English soldiers were paid £5 for either the head of a wolf (then regarded as one of the great pests in Ireland) or the head of an Irish 'rebel'. The soldiers, being lazy, resorted to bringing to their officers just the scalps of the Irish. The system was so successful that it was introduced into the American colonies where colonists were paid to bring in the scalps of Indians. The Indians thought this had a religious symbolism and copied it to acquire the white man's medicine. White man's history in America now claims 'scalping' as a barbaric Indian custom.

All the land east of the Shannon, once the Irish had been removed into their 'reservation', was to be parcelled out to capitalists, who had financed the conquest of Ireland, and to soldiers and other settlers who would create a 'New England' in Ireland. The Irish nation was to be squeezed until it no longer existed.

This is not considered 'remote history' in Ireland. Two of my own ancestors, Patrick and Stritch Ellis, were ordered to 'transplant' to Connaught. Stories of their deprivation and hardship were handed down in our family. However, they survived the trauma; tens of thousands did not. It is also easy to blame the personality of Cromwell. But the policy was first devised during the reign of the Catholic Queen Mary Tudor and enacted on a small scale in Leix and Offaly. Under Elizabeth I the policy was revived and tentatively tried out in Munster. From 1608, James I pursued the policy with results that echo today in the province of Ulster. Cromwell re-adopted the policy as a 'final solution'.

The Irish scholar, Ruairí O Flaithearta (1629-1718), wrote from Connaught: 'I live a banished man within the bounds of my native soil; a spectator of others enriched by my birthright; an object of condoling to my relations and friends, and a condoler of their miseries.'

To ensure the Irish were obeying the orders, on March 9, 1655, Charles Fleetwood, Lord Deputy and Commander-in-Chief of the English occupation forces in Ireland, ordered that all the passes over the Shannon, between Jamestown and Sligo, were to be closed, so that the area of Connaught and Co Clare was blocked off by military. Then he ordered a general search for all Irish who had remained east of the Shannon with obvious results. Along every road hanging bodies could be seen bearing placards: 'For Not Transplanting'.

Only the Restoration of the Stuart monarchy in England halted the worst excesses of the Cromwellian conquest. The wound runs deep and can never be repaired until the Irish nation, as a whole, is allowed to exercise its right of national self-determination. The story goes that an English news-reporter coming on a gunfight between English soldiers and the IRA on the Falls Road in the early 1970s, asked an old man who was standing nearby: 'When did it start?' The old man replied: 'When Strongbow invaded Ireland.' Perplexed, the reporter pressed on: 'When do you think it will finish?' The old man did not hesitate: 'When Cromwell gets out of hell!'

[*Historian and novelist, Peter Berresford Ellis is the author of* Hell or Connaught! The Cromwellian Colonisation of Ireland 1652-1660, *first published by Hamish Hamilton, London, 1975, and in paperback by the Blackstaff Press.*]

For Jonathan

The Clearing was first performed at the Bush Theatre, London on 17 November, 1993 with the following cast, in order of appearance:

KILLAINE FARRELL	Anna Livia Ryan
PIERCE KINSELLAGH	William Houston
SOLOMON WINTER	Michael O'Hagan
SUSANEH WINTER	Linda Bassett
ROBERT PRESTON	Adrian Rawlins
MADELEINE PRESTON	Susan Lynch
SIR CHARLES STURMAN	Stephen Boxer
A COMMISSIONER OF TRANSPLANTATION	} Alan Perrin
A SAILOR	
AN APPEAL JUDGE	

Directed by Lynne Parker
Designed by Francis O'Connor
Lighting by Paul Russell
Sound by Simon Whitehorn
Costumes by Joanne Kissack

The Clearing is set in County Kildare, Ireland.

By 1650 Cromwell had suppressed most of Ireland, leaving it in ruins. In 1652 the English parliament passed some of the most dramatic measures in its history: the policy known as 'to Hell or Connaught'.

Act One and Act Two: Autumn 1652

Act Three: Christmas 1653

Act Four: Summer 1654

Act Five: Autumn 1655

ACT ONE

Scene One

By a chestnut tree in the garden of a Manor House, County Kildare.

It is night. There is a strong wind blowing and the sound of wolves howling.

A girl (KILLAINE) is crying. Barely visible, a man (PIERCE) approaches.

PIERCE. Killaine Farrell.

She freezes.

Tell me it's not for Maddy O'Hart and I'll give you the broadest hug you've had since Christmas.

KILLAINE (*a smile of realisation*). Come here then.

They embrace.

PIERCE. Thank God. Thank God.

They break from each other, embarrassed.

So it's born.

KILLAINE. Nearly. But I had to come away. I've watched the pain changing her face and stood within the throes of life so long that I'm all filled up with human thoughts and I had to come and give them to the air.

PIERCE. It's strange to see you weeping. You always did seek a lonely spot to lick your wounds.

KILLAINE. I'm not weeping. Not now.

PIERCE. You should go back in before the wolves claim you.

KILLAINE. They won't come near.

PIERCE. They're near already. There's a misty breath about the house and a ring of yellow eyes, they're watching and waiting. They know it's nothing natural being born in there tonight.

KILLAINE. That's a wicked thing to say.

PIERCE. An Irish mother and an English sire, I'd say it again.

KILLAINE. A little child. With arms and feet and fingers.

PIERCE. And poison in its veins. It's a mixture to poison any creature.

KILLAINE. Then half the children hereabouts are ailing.

PIERCE. And I'd send them all to the devil if I could, the old ones and the young ones, all the bastards from Cromwell's kind. No good will come of one so sick.

KILLAINE. Don't talk like this, you frighten me.

PIERCE. Frighten you? I'd like to frighten you. I'd like to frighten all you people with your births and your weddings and your sweet songs. There's half the country dead.

KILLAINE. Pierce . . .

PIERCE. There's a village not half a day's ride from here where the people are crawling from want of strength and scraping corpses from the soil to eat. There are priests hanging from every post, the best men in the land bound and shipped to God knows where, but Maddy O'Hart can cling to her English squire and dance.

A cry of pain is heard from within the house.

What does that mean?

Perhaps you should go to her.

KILLAINE. They'll fetch me if she needs me. The place beside her belongs to her husband. I must be invited in. That's how it should be.

PIERCE. He's with her then?

KILLAINE. From the start. It's been hours now.

Pause.

PIERCE. Killaine, bring it out here for me. Where does she lie?

KILLAINE. Where the light is. She could see those woods from the window. At first she wouldn't be still at all and paced about and hung off the walls but now she's lying on a bed like a galleon, it has red curtains and white sheets that twist round her feet and onto the floor. There's a nurse there . . .

PIERCE. Mrs Ryan?

KILLAINE. No an English nurse, but she's right enough. And he, he kneels beside her and bathes her forehead, whispers to her and she grasps his hands with her white bones till the rings cut into his fingers. Poor Robert, he's one for smiling. I've never seen him so discomposed.

PIERCE. If he knew her as we do he wouldn't fret. Her mother died bringing her into the world and it's the two lives she has in her. Plenty to spare for a little one.

KILLAINE. Yes. Plenty to spare for a little one.

Pause.

He's a good man, Pierce, and I've never seen such care as there is between them. They drown in each other. It's a deep and watery love they have.

PIERCE. I'll go now. I've not been at the farm for two days. Get yourself inside.

KILLAINE. Will you come and see the child? She'll ask for you.

PIERCE. No.

KILLAINE. Don't forsake her, Pierce.

PIERCE. She doesn't need me.

KILLAINE. We're her oldest friends. What will I tell her?

PIERCE. Tell her I'll die before I knock upon his door. She seems to . . . you seem to forget, Killaine, my father and brother were killed by him and his kind.

KILLAINE. I don't forget. I don't forget. I've lost people too.

PIERCE. Then why are you here? You don't need to tell me. Maddy O'Hart, Maddy O'Hart . . .

If I could see her, I would . . . God knows I would see her, but . . .

Pause.

KILLAINE. I wish I could help you, Pierce. But your heart's so clenched and it's only you can loose it.

PIERCE. Go inside now. She'll want you there.

> KILLAINE *does not move.* PIERCE *looks at her for several seconds, then leaves.* KILLAINE *looks up at the tree. There is another cry from inside the house. She suddenly rips a piece of cloth from her skirt and ties it around a branch, then puts her arms around the trunk and closes her eyes.*

Scene Two

In the drawing room of the Manor House, the following day.

SOLOMON *and* SUSANEH *are waiting. She looks tense and angry. There is the strained silence which follows cross words.*

Footsteps approach.

SOLOMON. Here he is.

> ROBERT *enters, pausing in the doorway.*

ROBERT. Dear friends.

SOLOMON. We came as soon as we heard.

> ROBERT *goes to* SUSANEH *and presses her hand.*

ROBERT. Susaneh.

SUSANEH. Congratulations Robert.

> *He crosses to* SOLOMON.

ROBERT. Solomon.

SOLOMON. Here, let me embrace you. A hand isn't enough today, we'll do it the Irish way.

Your father would have been proud of you.

ROBERT. Yes. Yes, I think he would.

SOLOMON. And what is it you've got?

ROBERT. A boy. A promising boy.

SOLOMON. I knew it. I knew you could make a boy between you, didn't I say so, Susaneh?

ROBERT. I couldn't have hoped for so much.

SOLOMON. Have you given him a name?

ROBERT. Not yet. Madeleine wants to look at him a while. She thinks to read his name in his eyes.

SOLOMON. So she will if she says so.

SUSANEH. How is your wife?

ROBERT. Remarkable. She's resting now.

I tell you, Solomon, I've seen men perform some brave and steely acts but I've never seen a body turn itself inside out with effort as my wife did last night.

I shall look at women differently from now on.

I take my hat off to you Madam, and all your sex.

SOLOMON. You saw the little creature born then?

ROBERT. I did. Madeleine wanted me there and I wouldn't have left.

SOLOMON. God bless us.

My three youngsters appeared out of nowhere, isn't that right Susaneh? Dropped like birds down the chimney. That's what she would have me believe. I was never allowed to watch.

SUSANEH. Indeed you were not.

SOLOMON. There you are, you see?

ROBERT. It's a changing experience . . .

I feel almost religious today. Let's put a stop to it. Will you drink his health with me?

SUSANEH. We can't stay long, Robert.

SOLOMON. Just one drink?

SUSANEH. It's early yet.

ROBERT (*seeing something wrong*). Later then perhaps.

SOLOMON. Yes, yes. Later.

Pause.

ROBERT. I heard wolves last night, Solomon. I thought you were hunting yesterday.

SOLOMON. So I was. A bitch and three cubs. We could have done with your speed though, the place is alive with them.

ROBERT. I'll be out next time.

SOLOMON. My foreman says there's a public hunt been organised at Kilcullen. He was pushing me to do the same. Six pounds reward for a bitch's head, he tells me.

ROBERT. That's generous.

SOLOMON. It's a lot of money to any man in these times. I was thinking, if you'd lend your weight, we might organise something of the kind. There's some shifty hunters amongst our men and it would give them the chance to make a bit of something for themselves.

ROBERT. It would certainly get numbers down.

SOLOMON. Lord knows I've been able to pay them little enough these last few years. It's been a tinkling few coins I've handed over at payday and my eyes have sought the floor with the shame.

Ah well, at least I shall be able to feed them now the harvest's in.

ROBERT. I saw that your barns are full.

SOLOMON. Oh yes, I started early.

ROBERT. You started the same time as I. You know I follow your every move. One day I'll learn your secret.

SOLOMON. There's no secret. I wouldn't know a secret. Hard work, that's all it is. I don't mind admitting though, I've surprised myself this time.

ROBERT. You should put a guard on, Solomon.

SOLOMON. So I'm told, so I'm told. But if people come stealing, they must be needy and I've more than a little to spare. It's a fine harvest. It looks as though Cromwell did me a favour when he burnt my fields. I shall have to invite him back next year.

SUSANEH. How can you talk such nonsense?

SOLOMON. Now then Susaneh.

SUSANEH. How can you sit and talk such nonsense when you know what's coming?

A fine service to let you grow your crops so that he can come and take them from you.

ROBERT. What's this?

SUSANEH. Tell Robert what your brother writes.

SOLOMON. No. I've told you I will not tell him. Today is not the day for such news.

SUSANEH. Tell him, Solomon Winter, or so help me I'll tell him myself.

Pause.

ROBERT. Solomon?

Nothing can touch me today.

SOLOMON. I've had a letter from my brother in Bristol. He says they've passed laws.

SUSANEH. Laws to take our home away.

ROBERT. What do you mean?

SOLOMON. They plan to take the land from all of us who supported the King. And from the Irish who fought for the confederacy.

SUSANEH. You have heard nothing of this?

ROBERT. Take your land and put you where?

SOLOMON. I don't know. There's talk of Connaught.

ROBERT. I think your brother must be wrong.

They would move thousands?

SUSANEH. These are the men who killed a king. Nothing is beyond them.

ROBERT. When does he say these laws were passed?

SOLOMON. Last month.

ROBERT. Then why haven't we heard of it before?

We would have been told.

SOLOMON. Not if they're holding back. There are still Irish soldiers not dead or banished. I don't think they'll publish until Ulster's fallen.

Pause.

My brother is a cautious man; he wouldn't write this without good reason.

ROBERT. Then we must go to the Governor and ask what it means.

SUSANEH. That's what I said.

SOLOMON. Perhaps.

ROBERT. We must. I'm sure it is imagination, but I think we must go and put your minds at rest. Yes?

Pause.

SOLOMON. It would seem the thing to do.

SUSANEH. Thank you, Robert.

SOLOMON. I'm sorry to bring such news today.

ROBERT. No, no. Don't be sorry. You were right to tell me.

SOLOMON. They won't touch you, Robert. You never declared either way. But we'll be some of the first to go.

SUSANEH. I'm going nowhere.

SOLOMON. Susaneh . . .

SUSANEH. I didn't want to come to this country but I did come and this place is my home now and it is my children's home. If they want us out of Rathconran House they must pick us up and carry us.

SOLOMON. Yes, to the gallows, that's the way it will be.

ROBERT. No. No talk of gallows. Please. You're far too early with your talk of gallows. You know how quick a rumour is to light . . .

SOLOMON. They need to pay the army for their bloody work here, and the London merchants who gave to the cause. They have no money. What better way to do it than with land? Divide the sorry carcass that is Ireland now.

Pause.

ROBERT. We'll go to the Governor tomorrow. I know Sturman. If he's there, he'll see us.

SOLOMON. You can't leave Madeleine at a time like this.

ROBERT. Madeleine will understand.

We'll sort this out.

SOLOMON. What a country.

We sat in bed last night, the pair of us, holding hands.

Just when you think it's over . . .

SUSANEH. How did you think to christen the child?

ROBERT. In the Catholic way, I suppose. We were married in a Catholic church.

SUSANEH. I'd think again if I were you. I would give him a good Protestant christening. Not because of my faith. It will soon be as dangerous to be a Catholic here as it is to be a Catholic Priest.

MADELEINE *appears in the doorway. She is holding the baby.* KILLAINE *hovers behind her.*

MADELEINE. If that's politics you're talking, you had better stop now.

SOLOMON. Madeleine.

ROBERT. Madeleine, what are you doing here?

MADELEINE. The voices drifted upwards. I had to show this scrap to Solomon and get his opinion.

SOLOMON. Madeleine, just look at you.

MADELEINE. I hope you weren't thinking of sneaking away without a word to me.

SOLOMON. We thought you were sleeping.

ROBERT. She should be.

MADELEINE. I've slept enough.

SOLOMON. So this is the new Preston. He's beautiful.

MADELEINE. You don't have to lie to me. He looks like something that decorates a crypt. Hardly human at all. I hope he improves.

ROBERT. There speaks a true mother.

SOLOMON. He'll be as handsome as his parents, I'm sure.

SUSANEH. Congratulations Madeleine.

MADELEINE. Thank you Susaneh.

SUSANEH. He's a fine boy.

SOLOMON. We came as soon as we heard.

MADELEINE. I knew you would. I just couldn't bear to sit upstairs and hear you leave.

How are you both?

SOLOMON. Well. Well enough.

ROBERT. Now will you tell them goodbye and go back to your bed.

MADELEINE. I'm not sick, Robert.

ROBERT. You see how little she heeds me?

Killaine, can you make her go?

KILLAINE. No, Sir.

SOLOMON. Killaine knows better than to try, don't you?

MADELEINE. I can't go now anyway; I've used my last breaths getting down here and I'm so exhausted I'm afraid I'll have to stay a while.

SOLOMON. She's mischief all over.

ROBERT. I'll carry you then.

MADELEINE. Oh no. No need for such a spectacle. We'll just sit here, we won't cause trouble.

SUSANEH. We must go, Solomon.

MADELEINE. Susaneh, I'll be coming to you for advice. I know nothing about children. Killaine here had a handful of sisters but I'm sure we've a lot to learn.

SUSANEH. It's not difficult. He has his needs and he'll let you know them.

You have a nurse?

MADELEINE. I had thought to let her go.

SOLOMON. Has he told you his name yet?

MADELEINE. No, but I'm watching carefully.

SOLOMON. And will it be an Irish name or an English name, I wonder?

ROBERT. Whatever suits him best. Perhaps we'll give him one of each and let him choose.

SOLOMON. There'll be trouble in this house before that's decided.

SUSANEH. Solomon.

MADELEINE. You're not going already? I'll think it's something I've done.

SUSANEH. Robert's right. You need to rest. You haven't just yourself to think of now.

MADELEINE. I can't lie down any longer, I promise you. I'm singing all over. I've never been so happy in my whole life.

SOLOMON. You're a good girl Madeleine. I'm pleased for you. Pleased for you both.

MADELEINE. I wouldn't have said that last night, mind. I'd have been happy if I'd never seen him again. And I was expecting a girl. I had thoughts about a girl.

SOLOMON. You're not trying to tell me you're puzzled by a boy?

MADELEINE. No. But I suppose now he'll have to be taught to fight and watch his back.

SUSANEH. He could do worse than learn to defend himself, especially in this land. Don't pour scorn on the brave. Solomon fought and he'd fight again for a cause he believed in.

ROBERT. Madeleine only means she knows little about those things.

MADELEINE. I meant I would wish a different fate for a child of mine.

I didn't mean to offend you, Susaneh.

SOLOMON. We know you didn't.

SUSANEH. Will you come with us to the door, Robert? I would talk some more.

ROBERT. Of course.

SUSANEH. Madeleine.

MADELEINE. Susaneh.

SUSANEH *and* ROBERT *leave.*

SOLOMON. Forgive her. She didn't sleep last night.

MADELEINE. Is there something wrong, Solomon?

SOLOMON. No, no. Nothing at all. We'll call again soon.

MADELEINE. Thank you. Thank you for coming today.

SOLOMON. Tabhair aire di, Killaine. [Take care of her, Killaine.]

KILLAINE. Maith go leor. [I will.]

SOLOMON *leaves.*

MADELEINE. She disapproves. I don't think we shall ever be friends.

KILLAINE. She'll grow towards you in her time. But you go ahead of her and she can't follow.

MADELEINE. Is that what it is? I don't know, Killaine. I want to behave like the devil's own daughter when she's by me. The gaze she fixes on me . . .

KILLAINE. People aren't themselves, Maddy. It's a strange time. There's many who've forgotten to smile lately.

MADELEINE. Good patience. Why can't I learn from your good patience? I keep hoping a little will creep into me.

KILLAINE. You waited patiently for him.

MADELEINE. I had no choice. If I could have produced him after a month I would have done.

KILLAINE. I can't hold onto it; he's outside. He was inside you all that time, we listened for the beat of him, felt him trying out his limbs and now he's outside, for all the world to see.

MADELEINE (*holding him out to her*). Here.

KILLAINE. I might wake him.

MADELEINE. I hope you do. I hope he does more than sleep all day.

KILLAINE *takes the baby. She breathes him in.*

KILLAINE. Soft and warm. So soft and warm.

Pause.

MADELEINE. Do you remember that lamb we put a bonnet on and carried round in a blanket?

KILLAINE. And surprised people when they came to dote.

MADELEINE. We only stopped when it got too heavy. It was practically a sheep by the time we let it be.

He looks snug with you.

KILLAINE. I love him, Maddy. I'll love him as my own.

MADELEINE. I know you will.

You're to be his Godmother.

KILLAINE. No. That's for a fine English lady.

MADELEINE. That's for you.

KILLAINE. What have I got to give him?

MADELEINE. Everything you give me.

KILLAINE. But he'll be a little gentleman. Far above me. Robert won't want his son to have a servant beside him.

MADELEINE. Are you teasing me with your 'servant'?

KILLAINE. I don't mind, Maddy.

MADELEINE. Fine English ladies have companions. You're my companion and be sure to tell anyone who asks. Servant!

It's been a year now, Killaine. Have Robert or I ever done anything to make you feel unwelcome?

KILLAINE. No. You've been kindness itself.

MADELEINE. We want you here. I wouldn't have come without you. I need you.

Why do you smile?

KILLAINE. Your heart had set its course and you had the wind behind you.

MADELEINE. I wouldn't have come without you.

I haven't changed, Killaine.

KILLAINE. I know.

MADELEINE. Come on. Let's take the lamb outside and wake him up. He hasn't seen the sunlight.

They start to go.

KILLAINE. Maddy. Bhi Pierce anseo. [Pierce was here.]

Scene Three

In the drawing room that night.

MADELEINE *is sitting over the cradle, singing.* ROBERT *is attending to business at his desk. He stops and watches her for a few moments.*

MADELEINE. Anois a leanbh ta'd fabhrai trom,
    Is coir duit dul i bhfad o shin,
    I bhad 's is mian leat dul a stor,
    Mo shearc, mo leanbhin, a stor.

Sung to the tune of 'Caoinleach Glas an Fhomhar'

[Now little child, your eyelids are heavy,
And you may travel as far as you will,
And you may travel as far as you want to,
Now little child, now little child . . .]

He's almost there.

ROBERT. Are we alone? Where's Killaine?

MADELEINE. Walking.

ROBERT. It's dark.

MADELEINE. Killaine's afraid of people, not wolves.

ROBERT. Madeleine?

MADELEINE. It's strange to think we'll know him for the rest of our lives. A new friend.

ROBERT. Madeleine?

MADELEINE. Yes?

ROBERT (*smiling*). Come here.

She goes to him.

I thought you didn't like him.

MADELEINE. I never said that.

I can't take my eyes from him.

ROBERT. You used to say that about me.

MADELEINE. He has the edge with his being new.

ROBERT. Listen.

MADELEINE. I don't know if I like that 'listen'.

ROBERT. I have to go to Kildare.

MADELEINE. Why?

ROBERT. Solomon's heard some troubling news.

It's worrying Susaneh to sickness.

MADELEINE. What news? I knew there was something wrong.

ROBERT. You don't need to know.

MADELEINE. Robert . . .

ROBERT. Because I'm sure it isn't true. I'm going to take him to the Governor and see if he can explain it.

MADELEINE. When do you have to go?

ROBERT. Dawn.

MADELEINE. Tomorrow? Tomorrow?

ROBERT. I'm sorry.

MADELEINE. How can you leave him when he's just arrived?

ROBERT. I know. If it wasn't for Solomon I wouldn't go.

MADELEINE. If it wasn't for Solomon I wouldn't let you go.

ROBERT. You'll be all right. You've got Killaine and him to play with. And if you're really lonely, there's always Susaneh.

MADELEINE. I don't want Susaneh.

ROBERT. I'll take a couple of men and leave the rest. They can take care of things.

MADELEINE. I hate it when you're not here.

ROBERT. I'll be back as soon as I can be.

MADELEINE. Why can't he go on his own?

ROBERT. Madeleine.

MADELEINE. This is what comes of marrying a gentleman.

ROBERT. Meaning?

I'm as keen to investigate this as Solomon.

MADELEINE. Is that so?

ROBERT. Yes. And I want to help.

MADELEINE. Yes.

ROBERT. I don't like to see them so troubled.

MADELEINE. You put me to shame.

ROBERT. Three days at the most. I promise.

Pause.

MADELEINE. Well don't be amazed if you come home and he's speaking Gaelic and if he's chosen a name and it's Dermot or Eamonn or Tadgh.

ROBERT. I wouldn't expect anything less.

Thank you my love.

MADELEINE. We could come with you.

ROBERT. No. There's danger.

MADELEINE. From who? The English would greet you and let us pass and if the Tories rode down from the hills I'd ask after their mothers and they'd ride straight back again. We could travel safely to the tips of the land.

ROBERT. There's no 'safely'. Not anywhere. Don't ever imagine there is.

MADELEINE. Somewhere, there is.

I do know about the world outside. I might not let it in, but I do know.

ROBERT. You shouldn't have to know.

Pause.

MADELEINE. Killaine says Pierce was here last night.

ROBERT. Pierce Kinsellagh?

MADELEINE. He wouldn't come in.

ROBERT. They say he works for the Tories; he finds them arms and ammunition, gives them information.

MADELEINE. Is that what they say?

ROBERT. That's what they say. Do you think it could be true?

MADELEINE. I'm sure it is.

ROBERT. I see. Now I know the sort of company you kept before I tamed you.

MADELEINE. Tamed me? I set you free. And as for the company it was the best there is.

ROBERT. Better than me?

MADELEINE. No, not better than you.

ROBERT. You said the best.

MADELEINE. You pushed me to it.

ROBERT. What did he want, this Pierce Kinsellagh?

MADELEINE. He had heard my time was come.

It makes me sad, Robert. He was my friend, my brother. I dream about him sometimes. It's not even as if you fought for Cromwell.

ROBERT. Are you sure that's why he's angry?

MADELEINE. Why else?

ROBERT. I don't think Pierce would have a smile for any man you loved.

MADELEINE. What nonsense.

ROBERT. Oh, the innocence.

MADELEINE. I never encouraged Pierce that way. Except in childish games when we thought a kiss the beginning and the end.

ROBERT. Kissing now, is it?

MADELEINE. Stop it, Robert.

ROBERT. Let's start with a kiss then, and see where it gets us.

They kiss passionately. The kiss leads to an embrace.

ROBERT. Madeleine, Madeleine, I've got my Madeleine back.

MADELEINE. I was never gone.

Have I changed?

She takes his hands and moves them over her body.

ROBERT. Yes.

MADELEINE. Can you still love me?

ROBERT. No stills or wills or evers. I love you. Know it.

MADELEINE. I do. I do.

They sink into each other's arms and onto the floor. KILLAINE enters.

KILLAINE. Maddy, I've found blackberr . . .

Seeing them, she retreats and closes the door.

MADELEINE. That was Killaine.

ROBERT. It was the wind.

MADELEINE. It was Killaine. She'll mind.

ROBERT. How far can I go? How far?

MADELEINE. Only so far.

ROBERT. I think it's separate beds or I'll be mad by morning.

MADELEINE. No. You're leaving me tomorrow so you're holding me tonight.

As they embrace, we see KILLAINE running to the tree. She is holding the ends of her apron which is full of blackberries.

She recovers her breath.

KILLAINE. I found blackberries, Maddy.

We used to gather blackberries, way into the stumbling darkness. We didn't care if our arms were scratched or even our faces. Little purple fingers in the leaves. Then sometimes in the summer, we'd go down to the river and collect wet pebbles on the shore. And we'd take them home and my mother would say, why do you bother with those things, they're not pretty, they're not shells. She didn't know that every one was a tiny county or a town, depending on the size and the colour and the shape of the thing. Pocket size pieces of our country. And you could say, here, I'll give you Mayo and I could say, here I'll give you Meath and dream of a time when I would give you the whole world.

She suddenly climbs up into the tree, letting the berries fall. She shouts into the night -

Killaine's a fool. Killaine's a fool.

(*Quietly.*) A girl where she shouldn't be.

Pause.

If I could take more than two steps forward or two steps back . . . But I'm not that brave. I'm sorry Maddy . . .

In the house MADELEINE *and* ROBERT *are standing by the cradle.*

ROBERT. My every other thought is a wanting for him. I want him to have everything. I want to give him everything.

He will be happy, won't he?

MADELEINE. Oh yes.

ROBERT (*seeing her wet eyes*). Tears. Why?

MADELEINE. I don't know.

Because my mother never knew me.

Because we found each other in the middle of all this.

ACT TWO

Scene One

The Governor's office, Kildare.

ROBERT *and* SOLOMON *are sitting on one side of a large desk.* STURMAN *is standing on the other side. He has his back to them. He is a slight man, full of thinly disguised anxiety.*

He takes a long, painful breath.

STURMAN. This air is trying to kill me. It has passed through too many Irish lungs. Wet creatures, the Irish, wouldn't you agree? Full of tears and rain.

SOLOMON. They've had plenty to cry about.

STURMAN. You haven't been here long enough, Preston, to feel the effects of the climate.

ROBERT. Three years.

STURMAN. Three years. So many young men.

When was it we first met?

ROBERT. It must be nine years ago, Sir. I studied with your brother at Cambridge.

STURMAN. Ah yes. My father believed you led him astray.

ROBERT. And my father believed it was the other way round.

STURMAN. Too many liaisons.

ROBERT. We didn't think so.

STURMAN. And you, Mr Winter, how long have you had the pleasure of this isle?

SOLOMON. Almost thirty years, Sir.

ROBERT. Solomon's estate borders mine.

STURMAN. Yes.

ROBERT. You won't find a farm more prosperous in the whole of Ireland.

SOLOMON. A likely tale.

STURMAN. Profits are good then?

SOLOMON. They were before the troubles began.

ROBERT. You can understand perhaps, why Solomon is so
worried by this story of confiscation?

STURMAN. Oh yes, I can understand.

ROBERT. I have told him it is certainly untrue, but an idea so
devastating is hard to dismiss.

Pause.

I also thought you would want to know that such a rumour is
at large. It hardly contributes to the peace.

STURMAN. Where did you hear this information?

SOLOMON. From England, Sir.

STURMAN. From whom?

ROBERT (*seeing* SOLOMON *hesitate*). Solomon?

SOLOMON. I'm not sure I should say.

ROBERT. Of course you may say. It is not a crime yet, to write
a letter.

SOLOMON. From my brother, Sir.

STURMAN. In London?

SOLOMON. Bristol.

ROBERT. He has no connection with Parliament. He's a
farmer, am I right Solomon?

SOLOMON. Yes. An honest farmer like myself.

STURMAN. And did he too leave his honest fields to fight for
the King?

Pause.

SOLOMON. Yes Sir.

STURMAN. How unfortunate. You both chose the losing side.

SOLOMON. With respect Sir, there was no choice. A king is
put on earth by God. There was no choice.

STURMAN. There clearly was.

May I ask you, Mr Winter, what you would do if this information were true?

SOLOMON. Then it is true . . .

STURMAN. You see, I'm finding this rather difficult. A self-confessed enemy of the Commonwealth walks past my guards and into my office and demands to know if we have plans for those we defeated.

ROBERT. I was responsible for our coming here.

SOLOMON. I had not thought to be received as an enemy.

STURMAN. But why?

SOLOMON. I thought the war was over.

STURMAN. How convenient.

ROBERT. I'm sorry if . . .

STURMAN. I used to see darkness when I closed my eyes. Now I see the flash of a pistol being raised and aimed at me. Strange to think your hand may have held it. It may have been your chest I lunged at first when I drew my sword at Kilkenny. It may have been you who killed my father. Is that not so?

ROBERT. Sir Charles . . .

STURMAN. Is that not so, Mr Winter?

ROBERT. Solomon only fought for a matter of months.

STURMAN. A phenomenon is taking place in my office: I have two men before me, I direct my questions to one and the other answers. If the air were not so thick I would throw open the window and shout to the world to come and bear witness.

Pause.

Mr Winter?

SOLOMON. I did not fight to the end. A wound. But that is not something I am proud of. If I had been able to continue I would have done. If I could have stopped Cromwell whipping the blood from this country, I would have done.

STURMAN. And so you thought to go back to your farm, wash your hands and pick up your plough as if nothing had happened.

Those who start wars must expect to pay a price.

SOLOMON. We did not start this war.

STURMAN. Sixteen forty-one, the barbaric massacre of tens of thousands of English settlers . . .

SOLOMON. I am an English settler.

STURMAN. Then why did you escape?

SOLOMON. I had no part in sixteen forty-one, I joined a legitimate army to fight for my king.

STURMAN. You had a part. You had a part because you chose to join with murderers. You talk to me of whipping, but there were many innocent English souls who would have welcomed the touch of a whip. There were old men nailed to the gate-posts of their homes, women raped with knives then burnt alive. Do you know what it's like to watch someone burn? Their hair turning white, their mouths open, pieces of their flesh like snow on the wind?

ROBERT. Please don't implicate Solomon in this.

STURMAN (*to* SOLOMON). I implicate you.

Every single one of those murderers will be caught and tried and hanged until he is dead. Courts are being founded as I speak and their work will not cease until every single murderer is caught and tried and dead. And then, Mr Winter, we will deal with you and your kind. And if you escape with your life, think yourself fortunate.

He sits at his desk

In answer to your enquiry, Mr Solomon Winter, I will be joining the Commander in Chief in Kilkenny before the year is out, where a declaration will be made.

Good day.

SOLOMON *rises to go.*

SOLOMON. May God help us now.

STURMAN. The very prayer I utter.

SOLOMON *goes.* ROBERT *rises to follow him.*

Stay, Preston.

The door slams shut.

You do yourself no favours by bringing that man here.

ROBERT. I hadn't realised . . .

STURMAN. Hadn't realised what?

You find me changed, don't you?

ROBERT (*hesitant*). Yes, Sir.

STURMAN. In what way?

ROBERT. You have your duty to do, Sir.

STURMAN. Do not mistake me; there is a great deal of my heart in this work.

You sat beside me at dinner once.

ROBERT. Yes, Sir.

STURMAN. There was a lady in a lace dress. She sang. I turned the pages of the music.

ROBERT. I think I remember that.

STURMAN. I remember it as I remember dreams.

The responsibility of life and death, Preston; some of us must learn it. You may occupy your mind with matters of love and longing. We must watch the face of the world and sometimes change it too. You understand?

ROBERT. Yes, Sir. I think so.

STURMAN. Winter's is a dying breed. His notions of allegiance are extinct, the stuff of rhymes and fairytales. Kings may be appointed by the Lord, but so are the enlightened, the elect few. He would do well to learn that. We alone are capable of fighting the sins and corruption of the masses. We fight with divine strength. We cannot fail.

ROBERT. Is there a plan to confiscate land?

STURMAN. There is a plan for Ireland, and not before time.

Ireland is a whore. And whores cannot be trusted. She'll take the weight of any man, Spain, Holland, France, as long

as he can pay her. Even now there are reports of Dutch
ships off the coast. We will wrench her teeth out, one by
one. No one wants a toothless whore. Those who joined the
uprising will hang. Those who abetted with arms or shelter
will hang. Priests who consorted will hang. One hundred
and six prominent persons, whose names I have in my
possession, will hang.

Then we will flush her out. Those who joined the uprising
after sixteen forty-two, those who joined the Royalist army
or the so-called Confederate army, will lose their land.

ROBERT. Where will they go?

STURMAN. Far enough away for the security of the nation; I
hear Connaught is a desert. Perhaps an island off the coast.
They will be granted land equivalent to one third of their
former holdings and left to fend for themselves. Those who
do not obey, will hang.

ROBERT. And the land will be given to Cromwell's men?

STURMAN. Yes. In lieu of pay. And to others who proved
their loyalty.

We will rid the streets of surplus females and children by
shipping them to the plantations in the Americas. Cromwell
himself discovered the merits of such trade after Drogheda.
There is unlimited demand and tidy profits to be made.

ROBERT. You will meet with opposition.

STURMAN. Opposition in diminishing numbers.

ROBERT. And what of the Tories? Their ranks will swell.

STURMAN. We will hunt the Tories like wolves, and the
wolves like Priests.

Finally we will re-educate the whore in the ways of our
church, and the true ways of God.

Speechless, Preston?

ROBERT. I am only wondering if this is necessary, I mean, if it
would not be better to allow the native Irish to be . . .

STURMAN. Integrated? Should we integrate with drones? No.
It is both necessary and justified.

The Irish are devils, Preston. In truth.

There are many of Cromwell's men who swear they found tails on Irish corpses. Yes. They have an unearthly power to deprave. I have myself been forced to flog and dismiss several of my most trusted men for fornication with Papist sluts. You need only look at your friend Winter with his heathen hair and beard to know how they infect a soul. Is he not aware of the laws governing appearance?

ROBERT. I did not realise they were being upheld.

STURMAN. There seems to be much you did not realise.

I expect he speaks the Irish tongue.

ROBERT. I don't know.

STURMAN. You should make it your business to know when your neighbours are breaking the law.

Where is your discipline?

ROBERT. I have . . .

STURMAN. Or do you consider being a gentleman vocation enough?

ROBERT. No. I work hard.

STURMAN. At what? At what do you work?

ROBERT. My estate. It is beginning to prosper and I have planted a garden.

STURMAN. You should work at making this a safe and Godly land before you start with planting trees and shrubs.

Pause.

Your contributions to funds have been noted and greatly appreciated.

ROBERT. Thank you, Sir.

STURMAN. As too, was your hospitality to General Ireton and his men.

I take it your neighbour did not know of your guest?

ROBERT. I made no attempt to hide it.

STURMAN. And yet he did not know.

ROBERT. It was for one night.

STURMAN. And if we had need to avail ourselves of your hospitality again?

ROBERT (*hesitant*). You would be welcome.

STURMAN. Take care, Preston. There is another group of men who will lose their land: those who have not maintained constant good affection. I would hate to see your garden run to seed.

ROBERT. There will be no need of that.

STURMAN. Good.

Pause.

No more of this. I have found an appetite, a rare occurrence.

Will you stay and dine with me?

ROBERT. Thank you, but I must start for home.

STURMAN. Is there someone waiting for you?

ROBERT. Yes Sir . . . I have a baby son.

STURMAN. Excellent. You have married then?

ROBERT. Yes.

STURMAN. Do I know the lady? What is her name?

ROBERT. I don't think you would know her. Her name is Madeleine.

STURMAN. A Catholic name. Who was her father?

ROBERT. Her name is Madeleine O'Hart. She was raised by her uncle, Dermot O'Hart, after her father's death. He had land to the west of mine.

STURMAN. You surprise me, Preston.

ROBERT. If you met her you would understand . . .

STURMAN. Nothing. Believe me.

Pause.

You had better go to her then.

ROBERT. Yes.

ROBERT *rises to go.*

STURMAN. Constant good affection, Preston.

Scene Two

The drawing room, the following day.

MADELEINE *is admiring a piece of lace.*

KILLAINE *enters.*

MADELEINE. Would you look at this? Is it not the most delicate thing you've ever seen? Aunt Hannah brought it. She wants us to make a christening gown. Just look at it. You'll have to help me. I've no inkling where to begin.

KILLAINE *hands her a note.*

What's this? Where did this come from?

KILLAINE. It was nailed to the chestnut, the old tree at the back of the house.

Is that my name?

MADELEINE. Yes. And that's mine.

KILLAINE. It must be Pierce. He knows that's my place.

MADELEINE (*reading*). He wants us to meet him under the tree tonight. He'll be there after dark. Oh Killaine, he wants to see me. I'll take the baby and put him in his arms, he'll soften, I know he'll soften.

KILLAINE. There's something wrong.

MADELEINE. I've been thinking these last few days, I should go to him and say I'm sorry, tell him I know I'm a wicked kind of person, tell him I was bad.

KILLAINE. But you weren't bad.

MADELEINE. What does it matter? I want his friendship back. If I have to spend a few words to get it, I gladly will. They're of great value to him and scant value to me.

KILLAINE. How will we escape?

MADELEINE. What do you mean?

KILLAINE. Robert will be back.

MADELEINE. I'll tell Robert where I'm going. I won't go tip-toeing into the night as if I've a secret life. I want Pierce's friendship but I won't let him think he has a lover's pull on my heart.

What is it Killaine?

KILLAINE. There's something wrong. He wouldn't come here else.

MADELEINE. No. No, don't say that. He's coming back to us. Don't think it.

(*Holding out her arms.*) Come here.

(*She hugs her.*) How fragile you feel.

KILLAINE *breaks from her and turns away.* MADELEINE *watches her for a moment .*

You miss him as much as I do. It's my fault you're apart.

She goes to her and places the lace over her head, arranging it like a veil.

KILLAINE. Why do you do that?

MADELEINE. It's a beautiful bride you'll make, Killaine Farrell.

KILLAINE. No, Maddy.

MADELEINE. I know you'll soon have someone of your own.

KILLAINE. There has never been a man in my heart. You know that.

Pause.

I promise I'll leave you alone one day.

ROBERT *enters. He pauses in the doorway on seeing the two of them and a cloud passes across his face.*

ROBERT. What's this?

MADELEINE. Robert.

She runs to him and throws her arms around him.

MADELEINE. Oh Robert, I've missed you.

ROBERT. Steady.

MADELEINE. I hardly expected you so soon. Is Solomon with you?

ROBERT. No. I left him at Rathconran House.

Hello Killaine.

KILLAINE. Hello, Sir.

MADELEINE. You're hot.

ROBERT. We almost flew back. The horses are filling the yard with steam.

MADELEINE. I hope that wasn't on my account. Or rather, I hope it was.

ROBERT. We just wanted to be home.

How's my son?

MADELEINE. Thriving. Come and see.

ROBERT. In a moment. Let me catch myself.

MADELEINE. Here, sit down, I'll help you with your boots.

ROBERT. Has all been well?

MADELEINE. Grand. We can manage perfectly without you. And we've had so many visitors. Francis Gunn came to say he has a pony perfect for a little one to master. I told him it would be a while yet but I thanked him kindly for he means it as a gift. And him so thrifty. Then my aunt Hannah arrived with the prettiest piece of Flanders lace. Lord knows where she's been hiding it. (*Taking it from* KILLAINE.) Look. Such careful work. We're going to make a christening gown. She was sorry to miss you.

ROBERT. Where are you going, Killaine?

KILLAINE. Out.

ROBERT. It's too late for that.

MADELEINE. It's all right, Robert, she always . . .

ROBERT. It's not all right. I don't want anyone from this house walking about after dark. Not anymore. And there's to be no wandering barefoot in the woods and chattering Irish in the village. I want you to tell me where you're going from now on.

MADELEINE. Are there soldiers about?

ROBERT. It's just too easy for us to be unaware, unaware of the way things are moving. We need to be more careful.

MADELEINE. I had better not meet Pierce tonight then.

ROBERT. I'm serious, Madeleine.

MADELEINE. So am I.

ROBERT. You're seeing Pierce Kinsellagh? I go away for two nights and you're seeing him?

MADELEINE. He left us a note not ten minutes since and now I'm telling you.

KILLAINE *leaves.*

What's wrong, Robert?

ROBERT. It's frightening.

MADELEINE. What is?

ROBERT. There's a new mood growing in the town, in the whole country. It's darker than war, and more calculated.

MADELEINE. What does it mean?

ROBERT. It means madness.

MADELEINE. What does it mean, Robert? Is Solomon in trouble?

ROBERT. Solomon and Susaneh will have to leave their home. So will hundreds of others. Everyone who fought for the King and for the Confederacy.

MADELEINE. But they can't make people . . .

ROBERT. They can.

MADELEINE. Where will they go?

ROBERT. Somewhere beyond the Pale. Somewhere beyond what we know.

I should never have taken him there. I've made it worse. I thought I was helping him, I thought if we saw Sturman . . .

I don't know what I thought.

MADELEINE. You thought you were doing what was best.

ROBERT. It was foolish. Of course, Solomon won't say it.
He's trying to make me feel better. But we both know I
made a mistake.

Pause.

Perhaps you should see your friend Pierce tonight. If people
like him are caught, they'll hang.

MADELEINE. I see.

ROBERT. We'll be all right, Madeleine. But we'll have to be
careful. We mustn't make a sound.

MADELEINE. Of course we'll be all right.

Are you sure this isn't something that will go away? We've
heard before atrocious things are coming and they haven't
reached us.

ROBERT. I don't think this is going away.

MADELEINE. It might do. In a year we'll be living as we've
always lived. We'll forget we ever had this day.

ROBERT. I hope you're right.

MADELEINE. I am right.

Poor Robert.

ROBERT. Poor Solomon.

It might be as well to have the baby christened in a
Protestant church.

MADELEINE. Can't we wait a while and see . . .

ROBERT. We can't wait. Then they'll call us Anabaptists.
(*They smile together.*) We should do it soon, let it be known
in the village and hope it travels on the air, as far as Dublin.
As far as London.

MADELEINE. Whatever you say. I'm sure your God is as
good as mine.

Can Killaine still be Godmother?

Pause.

We can't stop breathing, Robert.

ROBERT. No. We can't stop breathing.

Scene Three

The drawing room at Rathconran House.

SUSANEH *is sitting very still with her hand over her mouth.*
SOLOMON *is waiting for her to speak.*

SOLOMON. Say something, Susaneh.

Pause.

SUSANEH. I will.

SOLOMON. You know I'll fight it, don't you?

Pause.

SUSANEH. Why were we put on earth?

SOLOMON. What's that?

Now, now. It will all come clear in heaven.

SUSANEH. Will it?

SOLOMON. But I do know one thing; we weren't put here to
hate, as that man hated me today. What am I? An ageing
bundle of flesh and substance. Nothing very remarkable.

I've fought with men and tried to take their lives, but I
haven't hated them.

Poor young Robert. He looked as pale as milk when he left
that office. I've never known him so quiet.

SUSANEH. Oh yes, poor young Robert. Poor young Robert
isn't going to lose his home, is he? I'm sure poor young
Robert has made very certain of that.

SOLOMON. Don't be too hard on him . . .

SUSANEH. Poor young Robert with his London ways. It's
time his fortune stopped. It's easy to win favour if you speak
in smiles and wanted words.

SOLOMON. He's gone out of his way to help us.

SUSANEH. Oh how can you be so soft?

SUSANEH begins to cry.

SOLOMON (*incredulously*). You're crying.

SUSANEH. Yes. Take a good look. Can I not spill and shake like any girl?

She sobs.

They're going to take our home.

They're going to take our home.

SOLOMON. Please don't, Susaneh. Don't cry. We'll fight it. I had no mind for skirmishing but now I see there's evil in it.

I'll take care of you.

SUSANEH. What has become of me? I was once, I'm sure I was, a kindly soul.

SOLOMON. You still are.

SUSANEH. No. All tightened up and taut inside. I wear my skin like rusted armour.

SOLOMON. No.

SUSANEH. Yes. Oh yes.

Pause.

SOLOMON. I should never have brought us to this.

SUSANEH. It's none of your doing.

SOLOMON. I should have kept my head down and let the war march by.

SUSANEH. No. It's a dear head and I'm fond of it but I'm proud of it too.

SOLOMON *takes her hand. They sit quietly for a moment.*

Our own kind. We would kneel and worship in the same church, and yet they look at us and see no more than animals. Animals to be herded here or there, here or there.

It's wrong, Solomon.

Scene Four

By the tree in the garden.

MADELEINE *and* KILLAINE *are waiting.* MADELEINE *is holding the baby.*

MADELEINE. The garden seems a forest in the dark.

KILLAINE. Stay close to me.

MADELEINE. He isn't here.

KILLAINE. He will be.

   MADELEINE *sees the cloth tied in the branches of the tree.*

MADELEINE. What's this? Is this a holy tree?

KILLAINE. I was making a wish for you.

MADELEINE. Sweet strange Killaine. You should make a
   wish for yourself.

   Pause.

Look at the house.

It looked like that the first moment I saw it. Robert led me
out of the woods, and there it was. All lit up. As bright as
angels. It thrilled me. I remember how hard it was to breathe
and the feeling of a pulse in my fingertips. I thought I was
looking at heaven.

   PIERCE *has entered and is listening.*

PIERCE. Killaine.

KILLAINE. Pierce.

Maddy's here. She's brought the baby.

   MADELEINE *and* PIERCE *look at each other.*

MADELEINE. So, Pierce Kinsellagh. You've finally come.

PIERCE. You don't need to whisper. We can't be seen or heard
   from here.

MADELEINE. It doesn't matter if we are. I want you to come
   to the house with us. Robert would like to meet you.

PIERCE. This is far enough for me.

MADELEINE. As you wish. I'm thankful to have you in my gaze.

I've missed you.

PIERCE. You may not see me again after today.

I'm going to the Tories. I can't stay in the open any longer.
I'll be dancing the hanged man's turn if I don't get out now.

But if you ever need me, go to my sister. She'll be able to
get a message to me. If either of you need me.

Pause.

KILLAINE. You're going?

He nods.

I'll kiss your face then.

He stoops so she can do so.

I'll think of you.

PIERCE. And I of you.

Sweet strange Killaine.

Don't go too near the wolves, now.

KILLAINE. Shall I take the baby, Maddy?

MADELEINE. No.

This is my son, Pierce.

Will you hold him?

PIERCE. No.

MADELEINE. Why? Because he has an English father?

PIERCE. Something like that.

MADELEINE. He has me in him too.

I'm sorry, Pierce.

PIERCE. For what? How can you be sorry if you don't know
what you've done.

MADELEINE. For upsetting you.

PIERCE. You didn't upset me. You . . . disappointed me.

MADELEINE. Is it so disappointing that I fell in love?

Can you not be happy for me?

PIERCE. When you climb into bed with the enemy?

MADELEINE. You make me sound like a whore.

PIERCE. Your words.

MADELEINE (*incredulous*). Why did you come here? To see if you could make me cry? I'm not a child now.

PIERCE. To tell you I'm leaving.

MADELEINE. You could have told Killaine.

I can't bear this. When I got your note, I thought of new beginnings . . . I thought we could be friends again.

PIERCE. Perhaps I did want to see you. Perhaps I wanted to see if I could recognise Maddy O'Hart in the English lady you've become.

MADELEINE. There is no English lady.

PIERCE. I see one.

Your father must be beating on the walls of Heaven.

MADELEINE. My father would be ready with his blessing.

PIERCE. Don't fool yourself.

MADELEINE. My father counted many English amongst his friends. He was glad to live beside them, as was your father once.

PIERCE. Before we knew their secret nature. Before we saw their true designs.

Pause.

You always did fancy queening it above the rest of us. Queen Maddy O'Hart.

MADELEINE. How hard you are.

PIERCE. I'm not the one who deserted my people.

MADELEINE. Oh Pierce, Pierce. Can't you try to understand? I'm not you. I don't see things the way you see them.

PIERCE. There was a time when we saw with the same eyes, when our hands felt empty, aimless, unless they held the other's. There was a time when I thought we would become one, not just our hands but our whole bodies, and we'd stay that way until we became three or four.

When we wrestled in the crackling heather, when we sat silent by the shore, that's what I was thinking, Maddy. That is what I thought.

Pause.

MADELEINE. I could never have married you.

PIERCE. Nor I you. I see that now.

MADELEINE. I want my life to be about joy . . .

PIERCE. I don't want your reasons. They don't interest me.

MADELEINE. We only have one life. I wish I could believe in the next, I try but I can't. And I feel my life, Pierce, to grasp and seize and swallow. I won't let it wither beneath a weight of hatred.

PIERCE. When I walk in a room, I have my father here, and my brother here. When I am asked a question, I hear their voices, loud in my ear before I answer. My life belongs to them and to my country, not to me.

MADELEINE. But it's your life. We could have been born at any time, in any place . . .

PIERCE. I was born here and now. I've seen what I've seen and heard what I've heard. All those things are in me. They are me.

MADELEINE. They're not.

PIERCE. They are.

MADELEINE. They're not.

They stop, realising the absurdity.

We see differently.

PIERCE. Yes we do.

She walks towards him until she is right in front of him.

MADELEINE. Do you recognise me Pierce?

Pause.

PIERCE. Yes.

MADELEINE. Will you hold him?

Will you?

PIERCE *is silent. She suddenly lets the baby fall and he catches it, on his knees in front of her.* KILLAINE *comes and puts her arms around his back.*

ACT THREE

Scene One

In the village. Christmas 1653.

Music. It has a Christmas strain but underneath it is foreboding.

KILLAINE is running. She is terrified, breathing heavily like a trapped animal. There is nowhere for her to go. She runs against a wall. A soldier enters, wielding a chain. A helmet covers the whole of his face. He advances slowly towards KILLAINE, who runs, almost throws herself into another wall. As he gets nearer, she freezes, no longer able to move. When he reaches her he pauses and then raises his arm high and strikes her across the head. She falls to the ground. He takes hold of her and drags her off.

Scene Two

In the drawing room in the manor house.

The room has been decorated with Christmas branches and candles, which MADELEINE is in the process of lighting. She is dressed in a splendid English-style gown and wears her hair up. ROBERT enters.

ROBERT. I'm going to the top of the woods to help with the felling.

You look beautiful. Everything does.

MADELEINE. I'm playing the lady of the manor. Am I convincing?

ROBERT. Very.

MADELEINE. Will you send a man back with some more green? I want the hall to smell of trees.

ROBERT. I will. (*Suggestively.*) Is there anything else I can help you with, Madam?

MADELEINE. Not like that. I know where you would help me to if you could.

ROBERT. A fine idea.

MADELEINE. And then nothing would be ready. Killaine's gone to the village to fetch the children.

ROBERT. Where's little Ralph?

MADELEINE. Preparing to meet his guests.

Nurse was trying to put a dress on his back but I told her, he's a walking boy now and deserves his dignity.

She thinks I'm meddling.

ROBERT. She should be used to it by now.

Will Killaine call at Rathconran House?

MADELEINE. They won't be coming, Robert. I went there yesterday.

ROBERT. You didn't tell me.

MADELEINE. I didn't want to worry you.

ROBERT. Are Solomon and Susaneh back?

MADELEINE. No. The whole place is shuttered up. I waited a while at the door before anyone came. It seems the children have to stay inside until their parents get back. Susaneh's afraid that if the whole family leave the house, soldiers will come and take it. I hardly think it's likely.

ROBERT. She's right to be wary. There are such reports about.

I thought they would be home by now.

MADELEINE. And I.

ROBERT. It hardly seems proper to be making merry while such a threat hangs over them.

MADELEINE. This is exactly what I thought, now.

What else should we do? It's Christmas. We'll help them, Robert. When there's something to be done, we'll help them.

ROBERT. Yes.

MADELEINE. I want this to be a special time. Ralph hardly
    knew a smile last year. This time he'll understand.
    Everything spread out before him, little hands to reach with
    and a voice that sings. I wish I was a child still.

ROBERT. Since when did you grow up?

They kiss.

I'll be back later.

MADELEINE. In time for the games?

ROBERT. Of course. I'm going to win all the prizes.

Scene Three

The Commission of Transplantation: Athy.

*On a raised platform, a man (the head Commissioner) sits
behind a large desk.*

SOLOMON *stands before him.* SUSANEH *is seated nearby.*

There is the sound of people talking in muted tones.

COMMISSIONER (*without looking up*). Name?

SOLOMON. Winter. Solomon.

COMMISSIONER. Of?

SOLOMON. Rathconran House, near Castledermot, County
    Kildare.

COMMISSIONER. On what date did you receive notice to
    transplant?

SOLOMON. November the fifteenth, sixteen fifty-three.

There is a pause while the COMMISSIONER *finds the
relevant paper.*

COMMISSIONER. You will please list for me all members of
    your family, servants and tenants who will transplant with
    you, also any numbers of livestock and any crops you intend

to take.

SOLOMON. None, Sir.

The voices quieten. The COMMISSIONER *looks up.*

COMMISSIONER. What's that?

SOLOMON. None, Sir.

COMMISSIONER. You have come here to register for transplantation?

SOLOMON. I have come here because I was required to do so by law. I would not break the law.

COMMISSIONER. You are also required to transplant to Connaught by May of the coming year. Is that a law you intend to break?

SOLOMON *hesitates.*

SUSANEH. It is a law we do not accept.

SOLOMON. Wait Susaneh.

Sir, I left a good farm in England to come here. The authorities there were begging folk to come, offering terms so favourable only a fool would have stayed. If you had heard the golden gains they spoke of, you would understand why a man might leave his . . .

COMMISSIONER. Mr Winter, I have no authority to hear appeals. I'm sorry. I am here simply to register those required to transplant. You received notice to transplant?

SOLOMON. Yes.

COMMISSIONER. Then you must register.

You are not obliged to leave immediately. You may have Christmas with your family in your own home. But you yourself must transplant in the new year and your family must follow before the end of May.

SOLOMON. We cannot go, Sir.

COMMISSIONER. Cannot?

SUSANEH. Will not.

COMMISSIONER. Then I am afraid I cannot help you.

Pause. SOLOMON *glances at* SUSANEH, *unsure of what to do.*

COMMISSIONER. If you leave this office now and do not return before the end of January, I shall be forced to issue a warrant for your arrest. You understand that? Any appeal you intend making will not be loudly heard from a prison cell.

SOLOMON. I may appeal?

COMMISSIONER. Once the relevant bodies are in place.

Everyone will have the right to do so, though I honestly believe most everyone will use it; barely a soul has passed before me this last month without muttering appeal. It will offer little hope should it become the general cry; somebody will have to go.

SUSANEH. And if we will not?

COMMISSIONER. The order is issued on pain of death, Madam.

SUSANEH. Perhaps that does not frighten me as much as you suppose. I have laid three babies in the ground; one for each that lived. I have glimpsed the freedom in their closing eyes and felt the warm peace waiting. I will do nothing on pain of death. Death holds no pain for me.

Pause.

COMMISSIONER. Please believe I find no joy . . .

I must advise you, in good faith, to register now and allow me to issue your certificate.

Pause.

SOLOMON. You are sure I may appeal?

COMMISSIONER. Quite sure.

SOLOMON. Then issue it.

SUSANEH. No Solomon.

SOLOMON. Yes. What else can we do? Would you have us start the year in chains? We must wait and then appeal.

SUSANEH. Do you not see the way they lead us? At every corner they will coax us just a little further, just a little

further on until we're on the road to Connaught, with
bleeding feet and our home in a cart. Think of the children.

SOLOMON. I am thinking of the children. I think I would not
see them orphaned. And neither would you.

Proceed, Sir.

SUSANEH. No.

SOLOMON. Yes. Proceed

COMMISSIONER. Very well. Let us begin with your family.
Please list all members of your family who will be
transplanting.

SOLOMON. Myself.

COMMISSIONER. Yes?

SOLOMON. My wife, Susaneh. My young son . . . and my two
small daughters.

COMMISSIONER. What age are you, Sir?

SOLOMON. Fifty years old.

COMMISSIONER. And do you have any distinguishing marks
which may be noted as proof of your identity?

SOLOMON. Distinguishing marks?

I have a scar on my back. On the right.

COMMISSIONER. Please remove your shirt so that the officer
may verify this.

SOLOMON. You mean . . . now?

COMMISSIONER. Mr Winter, do you wish me to issue the
certificate?

SOLOMON. Yes, Sir . . .

COMMISSIONER. Then remove your shirt. Please.

SOLOMON *glances at* SUSANEH. *He slowly takes off his
jacket and tries to unbutton his shirt but his fingers are
shaking and the buttons defy him.*

SUSANEH (*taking charge*). Here.

I suppose you will be branding us next.

Scene Four

In the woods at the back of the manor.

ROBERT *is standing by a fallen tree, chopping the limbs from the trunk. Through the sounds of swinging axes and the shouts of men,* MADELEINE *can be heard calling his name.*

ROBERT. Here.

She runs towards him, almost collapsing with fatigue and distress.

MADELEINE. Robert, Robert.

ROBERT. What is it? Madeleine? Is it Ralph?

MADELEINE (*through panting breaths*). Killaine. They've taken Killaine.

ROBERT. Who have? Who have?

MADELEINE. Soldiers. In the village. Soldiers with ropes and chains, pulling down the women and the children and Killaine. Oh God, Robert, they'll ship her to the Indies.

ROBERT. When was this? Who has told you this?

MADELEINE. A boy. A small boy at the door asking for his presents. A small boy with the world in his mouth. And then a running man arrived and said . . . Killaine . . . Oh God, Robert, he saw her fall.

ROBERT. Fall?

MADELEINE. The whole village is screaming.

We have to help her. Get her back, Robert, please get her back.

ROBERT. Do you know which way they went?

MADELEINE. No.

ROBERT. They could have gone miles by now.

Did they have horses? How were they moving the people?

MADELEINE. I don't know. I . . . loaded, he said they were being loaded.

ROBERT. Even if I find them, there's nothing to be done. I can't tackle soldiers.

MADELEINE. But they'll listen to you.

ROBERT. They listen to no one. Not even their commanders.
Not any more.

MADELEINE. Pay them. It's only Killaine you want. Give
them money, give them anything. They don't care who stays
or goes. Tell them you know the Governor.

ROBERT. No.

MADELEINE. But they're his men.

ROBERT. You don't know that.

Pause.

I'll go after them. I'll take you back to the house . . .

MADELEINE. No. I'm not going back. She's calling me,
Robert. You can't make me go.

ROBERT. Come with us then. But stay close. (*Shouting to the
men.*) Run back to the house and saddle the horses. Now.

What was she doing in the village?

MADELEINE. Bringing the children. I told her to go.

ROBERT. What fools we are. What stupid, blinkered fools.

Come on.

MADELEINE *is standing very still with her eyes closed, as
if listening to something.*

Madeleine.

They go.

KILLAINE's *voice is heard, singing in Gaelic, tremulous
and small. Gradually, it fades.*

Scene Five

In the manor house.

ROBERT *is standing in the drawing room, looking towards*
MADELEINE *who has stopped in the doorway. In another
room, the baby is crying.*

ROBERT (*gently*). Come in.

MADELEINE. We shouldn't be here, we shouldn't have come back.

ROBERT. Sit down.

There was nothing else.

We followed the wrong soldiers. It's dark.

We would never have found the other troop.

They're moving from village to village; there's no pattern in their progress. It's dark.

Go to the baby.

She doesn't move.

Oh my poor love. My poor love. I'm sorry.

MADELEINE. So what do we do now?

Pause.

ROBERT. It's very difficult. Perhaps she'll find her way back to us.

MADELEINE. How can she? Is there a road from Hell? We must discover where they are, if there's a ship. You must go to Sturman.

ROBERT. No, Madeleine.

MADELEINE. You can explain to him . . .

ROBERT. No. Now put it out of mind. I cannot go to Sturman begging the life of an Irish . . . of Killaine. He would surely believe I'd turned.

MADELEINE. Turned?

ROBERT. Don't you understand? You know how Solomon was met. It's only Sturman's favour now that's saving us from Connaught.

MADELEINE. And what's Connaught? Is it death, or slavery? That's what Killaine's in peril of, that's what we save her from.

ROBERT. Connaught is dangerous, Madeleine. You know it better than I. It may very well mean death . . .

MADELEINE. But we would be together.

ROBERT. It's a heathen place. No law . . .

MADELEINE. What does it matter where we are, as long as we're together? You and I, Ralph, Killaine? It's not so very far away.

ROBERT. I'll tell you what Connaught is. To me. Connaught is unthinkable. This is my land, my house and I will not give it up to go to some Godforsaken corner of this Godforsaken island. It was all my father left me. All I've got. Everything in England went to my brothers, if I went back there I'd have nothing. And I will not go to Connaught. I will not live there. It's different for you, you love this country but I do not. I love this little piece of it that's mine. That's all. This little piece with its garden and its fences and its big stone gates. We will not go to Sturman and we will not make a noise about this.

Pause.

MADELEINE. And Killaine?

ROBERT. Killaine will survive.

Pause.

I love you Madeleine. And I love Ralph. Go and lie down now. You're tired.

MADELEINE. Tired, is not what I am.

She leaves the room.

Scene Six

The Governor's office. Kildare.

STURMAN *is working at his desk.* MADELEINE *enters, quietly and unannounced. He looks up.*

STURMAN. Who the devil are you?

MADELEINE. Sir, you have my sister and I want her back.

STURMAN. How did you get in here? Who are you?

MADELEINE. My name is Madeleine Preston, Sir. You have my sister and I want her back.

STURMAN. Preston.

Where is your husband?

MADELEINE. He does not know I am here.

STURMAN. I'm sure he does not.

I'm afraid I will have to ask you to leave, Mrs Preston. I see no one without an appointment. You must return with your husband at a more convenient time.

MADELEINE. I have come with a civil request, Sir. I have been outside these five hours. If I leave now it will be too late.

Your men have taken my sister and I want her back.

STURMAN. Your sister?

MADELEINE. Soldiers. Snatching women and children to send them to Barbados. They are your soldiers?

STURMAN. How came your sister to be taken?

MADELEINE. She was in the village when they struck.

STURMAN. What was she doing in the village? Was she on foot?

MADELEINE. Yes, Sir. On foot.

STURMAN. Does she not realise the dangers? No lady would take such a risk.

MADELEINE. She has a home and a family who love her. She is Godmother to my son.

STURMAN. What is her name?

MADELEINE. Killaine. Killaine Farrell.

STURMAN. She is married?

MADELEINE. No, Sir.

STURMAN. Then she is not your sister.

MADELEINE. In all but name, we grew up together.

STURMAN. Ah; the famous Irish mist where lies become truth and truth, lies.

MADELEINE. Sir, Killaine is gentle and as light as air. I have walked behind her in the snow and been amazed to see her footprints. She would hurt no one, she troubles no one. She is not used to people and I fear for her. I am begging you to arrange for her release.

STURMAN. Out of the question. I cannot help you, Madam.

MADELEINE. It is such a simple thing.

STURMAN. I will not be seen to discriminate between one Irish wench and another. I will have my office full of nuisance and petitions.

MADELEINE. But I would tell no one.

STURMAN. Do not press me.

Who is taken and who is not is of no concern to me. In a perfect world you would all go.

MADELEINE. Give me a letter ordering her release. I will take it to the soldiers myself. You will never hear of us again.

STURMAN. Enough.

I must ask you to leave my office, Madam, or I will be forced to call my guards and have you removed.

MADELEINE. Where is she? Tell me where she is.

STURMAN. On her way to 'The Providence' in Waterford, I imagine. She may already be there.

MADELEINE. And she will be Barbadosed?

STURMAN. She will be shipped to the Indies, where she may hope to begin a new and upright life. Even the basest of men, trained up with sharp laws and hard labour can prove themselves good members of the Commonwealth.

MADELEINE. She will be a slave.

STURMAN. An indentured servant. She may be free in seven years.

MADELEINE. If she survives the voyage.

STURMAN. Indeed. I suggest you leave now; you may be there in time to wish her well.

MADELEINE. Do you have no sister? No daughter, wife? Do you have no mother?

STURMAN. Do not try me with naivety and arguments of care.

You people think you have a monopoly on heart. I understand love and I understand its limitations.

MADELEINE. It has no limitations. Only those you place on it.

STURMAN. God has compassion, yes, but He also has strength. God is no fool and neither am I. Good day to you.

She does not move.

Your husband will be angry, I think, when he learns you have been here.

MADELEINE. Do not pretend to know my husband. At least he understands the value of a life.

STURMAN. He understands what is required. He has worked well for us. A shame to have spoilt things with a reckless match.

MADELEINE. Robert has had no part in your doings.

STURMAN. You are too modest, Mrs Preston. He has made regular contributions to funds and provided practical aid on numerous occasions. But then, you must have known that. Or perhaps it is he who has been modest.

Pause.

MADELEINE. I don't know what I knew.

STURMAN. Please leave now.

He picks up his pen to work again. She does not move. She has her hand in the pocket of her skirt and is moving something in an agitated way, clasping and unclasping it.

MADELEINE. Will you take me instead of Killaine? I can bear it. She cannot.

STURMAN. You would leave your child? Your husband? Your country? Would you?

MADELEINE. Yes.

STURMAN. Would you?

I thought not.

Good day, Madam.

MADELEINE. Why do you good day me? I will not go.

STURMAN. Then I will call the guards.

Noticing the movement of her hand and growing pale.

What is that in your hand?

How did you get in here?

MADELEINE. Did I not say? I made myself invisible. I have powers, Irish powers. There is a witch crouching inside me. She was smothered by my little boy but now he's out and she's alive and kicking. I can send a dripping fog to hover on your head and send you mad with longing for the light. I can send a creature, a devil and an ape, to track your dreaming journeys and make your every sleep a nightmare. How unlike a pillow yours will seem, not soft enough to soothe your screaming skull. Powers and powers, oh such Irish powers I have. I would take care, if I were you.

She brings her hand from her pocket. STURMAN *is struggling to breathe now. He covers his eyes.*

STURMAN. Guards.

MADELEINE (*opening her hand*). What? Are you frightened of a child's toy?

She retreats silently and slips out of the door.

Scene Seven

The drawing room in the Manor House.

MADELEINE *is waiting anxiously.* SOLOMON *enters.*

SOLOMON. Madeleine. Thank God.

He shouts behind him.

It is her, Robert. She's here.

He goes to her.

They told us you were back but we hardly dared believe it.

MADELEINE. Is he coming now?

SOLOMON. Oh yes.

We've been straining our eyes for a speck of you these last two days. We were starting to fear we would never see one.

MADELEINE. I'm sorry you have had to search.

ROBERT *enters.*

SOLOMON. Look, Robert. Here she is. All safe and sound.

He doesn't move or smile even.

She had us frightened for a while, didn't she?

MADELEINE. Robert.

Pause.

SOLOMON. I heard about Killaine. It's a terrible business.

MADELEINE. It isn't over yet.

SOLOMON. Did you find any trace of her?

MADELEINE. I went to the Governor. He says she is on her way to Waterford. They mean to ship her to the Indies.

SOLOMON. God help her. I thought as much.

MADELEINE. It's I who will be helping her. I'm leaving for the harbour tonight. I'm only here asking Robert to come with me. And I need a carriage, or a change of mare.

ROBERT *does not look at her.*

SOLOMON. You can't go alone, you know, Madeleine. That's a ferocious journey, even for you.

MADELEINE. I'll be going any way I can.

SOLOMON. Perhaps I . . .

ROBERT. I don't know how to thank you for your help these last few days, Solomon.

SOLOMON. Not a word, now. It was done from love not duty.

ROBERT. You must go home and rest. I insist. You've hardly sat down since you got back from Athy.

MADELEINE. Were you seen by the Commission?

SOLOMON. We were. We had no choice but to register. But they say we may appeal so there's hope for us yet.

MADELEINE. I'm glad.

SOLOMON. It hardly seems important now.

What a country.

Cromwell has had a merry Christmas. Parliament has dissolved, they say, and handed every power to him.

Did you hear this?

MADELEINE No.

SOLOMON. Lord Protector of the something or other, that's what we're to call him. I said to Susaneh, it's a black day when we need his brand of watching.

ROBERT. Indeed.

MADELEINE *looks at* ROBERT *with a mixture of hope and disdain.*

SOLOMON. Well . . . I shall leave you to . . .

ROBERT. Yes. Thank you, Solomon.

SOLOMON. Call if you need me.

ROBERT. I will.

SOLOMON (*stopping in the doorway*). You're a brave girl, Madeleine.

He leaves.

Pause.

MADELEINE. I know you're angry with me.

ROBERT. Don't. Don't start being reasonable now.

MADELEINE. I'm sorry I left without telling you. It seemed the only way and I felt sure you would know where I had gone.

Why did you let Solomon go searching round the countryside . . .

ROBERT. I did not think you would be so stupid.

MADELEINE. I had to go. I couldn't sit or stand or sleep. I had to go. Surely you must understand that.

ROBERT. You saw him, then?

MADELEINE. Oh yes. As thin a piece of humanity as I ever hope to meet.

ROBERT. You angered him.

MADELEINE. He angered me.

All the way here I have been hoping and praying that you will come with me to Killaine. If you won't, I will go alone. But I must ask you for money, Robert. I can do nothing without that. And a carriage.

ROBERT. Do you realise what you have done?

Do you?

You do not anger a man like Sturman without you pay a price. This means transplantation.

MADELEINE. You don't know that.

ROBERT. It's as if I had the paper in my hand.

MADELEINE. I cannot talk of this now. I have precious little time.

ROBERT. What kind of wife are you? I tell you not to do something, beat out to you the danger it would put us in, Ralph in, and you run away and do it. I tell you everything is over, our whole life ruined and you say you cannot talk of it.

MADELEINE. Will you come with me to Waterford?

ROBERT. What kind of wife are you?

MADELEINE. I am an Irish wife.

ROBERT. And don't I know it.

Pause.

MADELEINE. I hope it was not that contempt which won your help for Sturman.

ROBERT. What?

MADELEINE. I'll be leaving within the hour.

ROBERT. When I helped him I had no contempt, only a will to survive. Do not expect me to apologise for that.

MADELEINE. Apology? I was hoping for a denial. May I have some money, Robert? Please.

ROBERT. No. You may not. You may not have some money.

MADELEINE. Robert, don't do this. Please don't do this.

My father left me money. And my uncle. Give me some of that.

Do you not care for her at all?

He does not answer. She heads for the door. He blocks her way.

Let me pass.

ROBERT. Where are you going?

MADELEINE. To say goodbye to Ralph before I leave.

ROBERT. Really? Ralph? I thought you had forgotten him. I thought he had drowned along with everybody else in your great love for Killaine Farrell.

MADELEINE. Let me pass.

ROBERT. You're going nowhere. Or if you go anywhere it will be with me, to Sturman, to apologise, to put right the damage you have done. Lady.

He pushes her. She falls. Silence. She is incredulous.

She puts out her hand to him, asking him to help her up. He walks out.

Scene Eight

On the deck of 'The Providence'. Waterford.

An armed sailor is casually patrolling the deck. MADELEINE approaches from the ramp that links the ship to the quay. The sailor sees her and draws his cutlass.

SAILOR. Don't move.

State your business.

MADELEINE. I want to see . . .

SAILOR. Irish.

MADELEINE. I don't mean trouble.

SAILOR. What else does Irish mean?

MADELEINE. I want to see a friend of mine . . .

SAILOR. This is a prison ship, not a Dublin ale-house.

MADELEINE. I think you have a girl on board . . .

SAILOR. Do we?

MADELEINE. A girl called Killaine Farrell. I want to see her.

SAILOR. Sorry. No visiting.

MADELEINE. I'll pay you.

I've come a long way. I have to see her.

SAILOR. You people don't have money.

MADELEINE (*taking a locket from around her neck*). I'll give you this.

SAILOR. I'd rather you gave me something else.

MADELEINE. It belonged to my mother. It's gold.

SAILOR. I'll decide that for myself.

MADELEINE. You'll get it when I've seen her.

SAILOR. I'll get it now or I'm not shifting.

She gives it to him. He examines it.

Still warm.

What's the name?

MADELEINE. Killaine Farrell.

SAILOR. Don't you move now.

He leaves for a moment and shouts in the direction of the hold.

Fetch up Killaine Farrell.

He returns.

MADELEINE. Is she on board?

SAILOR. There's three hundred of them down there. I don't know them all personally, if you understand.

MADELEINE. What's happening then?

SAILOR. I gave the name. We'll have to be patient and see what comes up.

Pause.

Last time I gave a name, four of them came. Scratching and tangling like a ball of cats. Thought they was getting a sniff of freedom. Turned out it was a hanging name, a name for the gallows they was so keen on owning. Lynched all four of them in the end. Couldn't sort the one from the other.

MADELEINE. Can a girl be got out?

SAILOR. What do you think I'm doing here?

MADELEINE. But if . . .

SAILOR. Do you not see the bars? The nets over the water? No one gets off here.

Don't you fancy coming then? You'd fetch a price at Bridgetown.

MADELEINE. I'm married to an English gentleman.

SAILOR. Is that so? You'll be in need of a man then.

Oh yes, I'd have no trouble shifting you. I know a man who'd find you useful. Buy you for the scullery and work you in his chamber. Up and down, up and down, up and down.

MADELEINE. Keep away from me.

SAILOR. I know you for the biting kind, I'm right, aren't I?

Well, there's ways and means of dealing with the biting kind.

MADELEINE. If I paid you, would you let her go?

I can get money.

SAILOR. Where from? I don't see your English gentleman in the vicinity.

MADELEINE. I'll give you my wedding ring.

SAILOR. There's an offer.

KILLAINE *is pulled from the hold by a crewman. She stands, staring at the ground, blinking as her eyes adjust to the light.*

SAILOR. Is that the one? Not much to look at.

KILLAINE *looks up slowly and sees* MADELEINE, *whose eyes have filled with tears.*

MADELEINE. I'm here. I've found you.

That's the longest trip to the village I ever heard of. Did you have stones in your boots? Ralph got quite cross.

KILLAINE *suddenly moves and turns away from her.*

Killaine.

SAILOR. She's mad, that one. Won't last the journey.

MADELEINE. Killaine, come here.

KILLAINE. Thug me gra duit, Maddy. Imigh anois. [I love you, Maddy. Now go.]

MADELEINE. I can't hear you.

Look at me. Just turn around and look at me.

Killaine Farrell, you look at me now.

KILLAINE (*suddenly*). Don't come here speaking my name, just when I've found the animal.

Don't speak my name.

Pause.

You shouldn't be here.

MADELEINE. Where else should I be?

We looked for you. Into the night we looked for you. Everyone. But we followed the wrong soldiers. I was so sure they were the right ones. Why didn't you call louder? Why didn't you call to me?

KILLAINE. Go away.

MADELEINE. No.

KILLAINE. Please.

MADELEINE. No, I won't go away. That's a fine welcome for a girl who's travelled half the country. And without a carriage. Where did you get your manners from?

MADELEINE *moves towards her.*

KILLAINE. Don't.

MADELEINE. What is it? (*Suddenly thinking she is injured.*) Show me your face. Show me your face.

KILLAINE. I'm dirty.

MADELEINE. Dirty? Sweet strange Killaine. Have you not washed me with your own soft hands and kissed the day from my face?

KILLAINE. I'm full of dirt.

MADELEINE. I don't understand what you mean, Killaine? You're frightening me.

KILLAINE. Inside.

A soldier.

One gritty moment on the ground. One gritty moment and I'm all gone. Do you know? Not so sweet and strange now. Just.

Pause.

MADELEINE (*to Sailor*). When do you sail?

SAILOR. Depends.

MADELEINE. When? Just tell me.

SAILOR. You'd better watch your mouth.

MADELEINE. I'm coming back with money. Have her ready for me.

SAILOR. I don't take orders from you.

MADELEINE (*to KILLAINE*). I have to leave you now but I'm coming back. I'm going to get money and pay them to let you go.

KILLAINE. I'm already gone.

MADELEINE. No you're not. You're coming with me.

KILLAINE. No.

MADELEINE. I'm going to get Pierce.

KILLAINE. No.

MADELEINE. He has to know.

KILLAINE. That's no. Promise me you won't tell him.

MADELEINE. I will promise no such thing.

What they have done to you . . .

KILLAINE (*shouting*). He'll hang.

Oh Maddy. I'm sorry. I'm sorry.

They embrace.

MADELEINE. Killaine, Killaine. I've missed you. Let me help you. Please. If I could go and get some money . . .

KILLAINE. From where? From Robert? I don't think so.

MADELEINE. Robert wants you home. He said to tell you.

KILLAINE (*laughing*). Poor Maddy. I always could see through to your soul.

She laughs some more.

MADELEINE. I don't see what's so amusing.

She stops laughing. They look at each other for a moment.

KILLAINE. It smelt of tobacco when they put us down below. So like your father. Do you remember? I could feel his hand on my head. And when I closed my eyes, you were there, very bright and perfect. But the smells are different now. And I've put you somewhere very deep, like a doll under my skirts. And I won't take you out until it's safe. Safe to remember. Do you understand? There are some things you can't change, Maddy. Even you.

MADELEINE *is crying and clinging to her.*

MADELEINE. I can't let you go.

KILLAINE. You can. You should.

Don't fret now. Don't fret. I'm taking the wolves.

She kisses her head and starts to go.

MADELEINE. Killaine. Have my ring. Sell it. I don't mind.

KILLAINE. It wouldn't last the night.

(*Smiling.*) I'd wake up in the morning without a finger.

MADELEINE *grabs her and hugs her.* KILLAINE *takes her hands.*

I love you Maddy. Now go.

ACT FOUR

Scene One

The Governor's office. Kildare.

STURMAN *and* ROBERT *listen as the town clock strikes noon.*

STURMAN. That is the first one hanged.

Let us drink.

To the destruction of our enemies.

ROBERT. The destruction of our enemies.

STURMAN. Perhaps now they will understand the meaning of a deadline.

This should have been started on the second of May. As was threatened.

ROBERT. Are there to be more hangings?

STURMAN. Every city will be searched. All those who have chosen to ignore the law will be hanged or transported.

A new deadline will be set for those such as yourself. March, I believe. Let us hope this time it is observed.

In my private moments . . . There are times when I question this desire to be merciful. It is a weakness. Those who come appealing, with indignation on their brows, should think again before they call us despots. Would despots offer land in lieu, the option of a new life overseas, would despots hear appeals? I think not.

Why do we not bury them in pits so deep that they will be forgotten? That is what I think in private moments.

We are making a rod for our own back.

Do you not agree?

ROBERT. I follow your reasoning, Sir.

STURMAN. Do you? But then you would have to.

Do not repeat what I have said.

ROBERT. No, Sir.

Pause.

STURMAN. Why do you come to me now with your apology?

ROBERT. I came before, Sir. The very week I received the transplantation order. I came several times but was told you would not see me.

STURMAN. Really? I must have been occupied. I will not accept your apology. You must have known I would not. I would not accept it from the lady herself.

This is not a question of civility, it is one of duty. I have seen her secret nature, Preston, and it is dangerous. You, I am sure, could not have seen it or you would not have taken her to wife.

Why did you marry her? If there were not sufficient virgins here, you could have cast your eye on London town.

ROBERT (*slowly and with difficulty*). She was unlike anyone I had met, Sir. Hers was not the dutiful love I had come to anticipate. It was given freely. She saw only the best in me.

STURMAN. And now? You said 'was'.

ROBERT. It is true that she is grown somewhat distant. It is six months now since the girl was taken, Killaine Farrell, and, well . . . it was a blow to her and . . . there is little charity between us and . . .

STURMAN. And?

ROBERT. There are other things. I am concerned for my son.

STURMAN. Other things?

Pause.

What do you want of me, Preston?

ROBERT. I have said, Sir. I came to apologise.

STURMAN. The very week of your appeal?

I think there is a motive in the timing.

ROBERT. I want to keep my estate. And to give my son a good life.

STURMAN. And what do you want of me?

Pause.

I will tell you what you want. You want me to intervene on your behalf. You want me to ensure it is your wife who is removed and that you be allowed to stay.

ROBERT. No, Sir.

STURMAN. Really? I think that is exactly what you want.

Well?

Oh dear, oh dear. It is a pity. I would have helped you, Preston. You are a fool, yes, but you are young and even I was given to folly in my youth. You should have been sterner, certainly, but you are not the first to fall; we have but pale defence against the darkness, especially when so far away from home.

ROBERT. Yes, Sir. I have felt myself in need of guidance.

Pause.

Is there . . . Is there any way that we may both be allowed to stay?

STURMAN. Do you mean to mock my generosity?

ROBERT. No, Sir.

STURMAN. Do I seem a man who can be pulled and pushed? Do you think me easy?

ROBERT. I did not say . . .

STURMAN. She is on your back still. I see her now. And you must throw her off before she brings you to your knees.

ROBERT. She is my wife.

Pause. STURMAN *suddenly goes to the door and opens it.*

STURMAN. Enough.

You are no use to me.

Pause.

ROBERT. If you were to help me, Sir, would I still have need to appeal?

STURMAN. You are extraordinary, in your way.

Even now you cast about for a sweet and silent passage.

It would suit you very well to send me whispering in ears, would it not? To emerge from this unpleasantness all perfect and unscathed?

Would you have need to appeal? Oh yes. I'm afraid you would. You would stand in court and speak the words and you would make your plea. You would be seen to be repentant and I, would be seen to be merciful. That is, after all, the order of the day. How illuminating it would be for all concerned.

Poor Preston; your very own reckoning.

Pause.

Now. What do you want of me?

Scene Two

In the garden of the Manor House.

It is a beautiful day. ROBERT *is sitting, watching* MADELEINE *playing with Ralph. She leaves him to play on the grass and comes and stands near to* ROBERT. *There is a strong tension between them.*

ROBERT. Poor little fellow; his spirit is stronger than his legs.

MADELEINE. Oh, he is an expert tumbler. It's as well he has the grass to catch him.

ROBERT. He's so affronted when he falls. Then his face crumples and the howls arrive. One minute he is a little man, the next, he is a baby.

MADELEINE. Sometimes I almost will him to upset himself just to have the joy of comforting him.

Does that sound bad?

ROBERT. No. It sounds like Madeleine.

Pause.

MADELEINE. We have a sweet child.

ROBERT. Yes we do.

She starts to go.

Madeleine, stay with me. Will you?

I have hardly seen you of late.

MADELEINE. You see me all the time.

Very well.

ROBERT. Come and sit beside me.

She is hesitant.

Just sit with me.

She sits down near to him.

I adore these midsummer days.

MADELEINE. And I.

ROBERT. It's hard to be angry with the world on a day like this.

I was watching you with Ralph. You know, there's a colour in your hair that only shows in the sun.

MADELEINE. A sort of red.

ROBERT. A sort of red.

Let's all three eat outside tonight, under the trees, as we used to. It would be peaceful for you.

MADELEINE. I would like that.

ROBERT. Would you?

MADELEINE. We'll miss the garden, when we go to Connaught. We'll never see its prime. I hope those who come after us are tender with it.

Pause. ROBERT *cannot answer.*

There's something I want to say to you. I want to say that I do care; about Connaught, about the appeal . . .

ROBERT. Madeleine . . .

MADELEINE. I have to say it now. When you went to Kildare, I knew where you were going and I pretended that I didn't care but I do and I see how you struggle with yourself and it's brave, Robert. I am trying to understand the past but you are trying to face the future and perhaps that is worse. I have been thinking perhaps that is worse.

There now; it is said.

I will take Ralph inside for his nap.

ROBERT. Madeleine.

He grabs her hand and pulls her towards him.

He kisses her.

MADELEINE. Don't Robert.

He persists, holding her tightly.

ROBERT. Yes. Madeleine . . . Madeleine I need you to help me.

MADELEINE. What? I've said all I can.

ROBERT. I need you to give me something. If you could just give me something, Madeleine.

MADELEINE. Stop it.

He is kissing her passionately now, his hands moving over her body. She stops struggling.

ROBERT. You see. You see. You see how easy it can be. You see . . .

MADELEINE (*suddenly pushing him very hard*). No.

He falls away from her. She moves away.

It was Killaine. I'm sorry. I'm so sorry. I feel so guilty.

ROBERT (*shouting*). Damn guilty.

MADELEINE. Ralph . . .

ROBERT. You will be sorry. One day you will look up and you will see what you have done and you will be sorry.

MADELEINE. I told you it was all that I could say.

ROBERT. Well it's not enough.

MADELEINE. What do you expect of me? I'm here aren't I? It almost kills me but I am here and I will go to Connaught with you but I cannot . . .

ROBERT. Cannot what? Touch me? Love me? Forgive me? Forgive me? What about my forgiveness? You move about enchanted with your own grief and you do not notice mine.

MADELEINE. Are you . . . are you saying that you grieve for Killaine?

ROBERT. No.

MADELEINE. What then?

ROBERT. I grieve . . . I grieve for us.

Pause.

MADELEINE. It's not that I blame you. I don't blame you . . .

ROBERT. It's all right.

MADELEINE. I think perhaps in time . . .

ROBERT. I said it's all right.

I expect too much of you.

She starts to go.

I will go to the appeal alone.

MADELEINE. When is it?

ROBERT. The day after tomorrow.

MADELEINE. I will come with you.

ROBERT. No. Your presence would be provocative.

MADELEINE. But we should face it together.

ROBERT. Plenty of time for that. I will go alone. We have more chance that way.

MADELEINE. Very well.

She goes to Ralph.

ROBERT. Very well.

Scene Three

The Court of Appeal: Athy.

ROBERT *is waiting in the busy entrance hall.* SUSANEH *approaches.*

SUSANEH. Good day, Robert.

ROBERT. Susaneh.

SUSANEH. Who were you expecting?

ROBERT. No one.

SUSANEH. I saw your name up on the board and came to wish you well.

ROBERT. How are you?

SUSANEH. Better for seeing a friendly face.

ROBERT. Are you alone? Where's Solomon?

SUSANEH. He has gone back to Rathconran House.

His health is very poor, Robert.

ROBERT. His health? I have not seen him this last month.

SUSANEH. We've all had things to think about.

We lost our appeal. Solomon took it badly, I'm afraid. I think his heart is breaking and it is such a large heart that it shakes him through.

ROBERT. I'm so sorry. You should have told me.

SUSANEH. I'm raising another appeal on the grounds of his illness. If I pester them sufficiently perhaps they will tire of me and beg me to do as I please.

ROBERT. They should listen this time.

SUSANEH. I doubt it. I just sat in court and heard Mathilda Carthy told to go. A blind old lady of almost ninety. I'm sure we'll all sleep soundly in our beds now such a threat has been removed.

It's politics that sways them, Robert. People aren't the thing.

You know they hanged a man in Dublin?

ROBERT. I heard it.

SUSANEH. Tied a placard around his neck, 'For Not Transplanting'. It is surely the beginning of the end.

You do not contradict me.

ROBERT. What, sorry?

SUSANEH. I am so used to having Solomon beside me. Optimists are priceless at times like this.

How is Madeleine?

ROBERT. Madeleine is fine.

SUSANEH. And Ralph?

He cannot answer and is close to tears.

I am praying for you. I'll watch from the gallery.

ROBERT. No. No, don't stay, Susaneh.

SUSANEH. But I intend to.

STURMAN enters.

STURMAN. I have kept you waiting, I think.

ROBERT. Not at all, Sir.

This is . . .

STURMAN. I know who this is. She makes her presence felt.

Good day, Mrs Winter.

SUSANEH. It may cheer you to learn, Lord Sturman, that my husband is very ill as a result of your persecution.

STURMAN. You are wrong to imagine that it cheers me, Madam. The information has no effect whatsoever upon my constitution. But thank you for the thought.

I wish you well in Connaught.

SUSANEH. I wish you well in hell.

STURMAN (*turning to leave*). Preston.

ROBERT. Don't stay, Susaneh. Please.

They go. SUSANEH watches them.

Scene Four

The Court of Appeal: Athy.

ROBERT *is standing before the* JUDGE. STURMAN *is sitting*

*to one side. There is an occasional murmur of voices from the
gallery.*

JUDGE. Do I understand you correctly?

You say it is your wife alone has shown us disaffection.

ROBERT. Yes, Sir.

JUDGE. And you wish her to be transplanted to Connaught
while you remain in your home?

ROBERT. I do not wish her to be transplanted but if she must
go because of her offence, I do not think it just that I should
share her fate.

JUDGE. But she is your wife, Sir, and your responsibility.

ROBERT. She is disobedient.

JUDGE. Disobedient? Come, come. If we were to exonerate
every fellow with a wayward wife, there would be no one
on the road to Connaught and no one likely to be.

No, Sir. You are as one in the eyes of the Lord; if she must
go then so must you.

ROBERT. I no longer wish to own her as a wife.

Pause.

Her behaviour of late has . . . we no longer live as man and
wife.

JUDGE. I see. For how long has this been the case?

ROBERT. Since the beginning of the year, Sir. It is over six
months now and we do not look each other in the eye.

If we went to Connaught, I do not think we would remain
together.

All I ask is that I be allowed to keep my son and to stay here
and give help to the proper government of this island, as I
have always done.

JUDGE. Sir Charles, you have something to say on this man's
behalf.

STURMAN. Indeed, Sir.

I know this to be a good man, a helpful and affectionate
man.

JUDGE. And yet it was yourself, was it not, who ordered the transplantation?

STURMAN. Because of his wife. She forced her way into my office, behaving in a most threatening manner, proving herself to be unruly and degenerate in the extreme.

I do not excuse Preston's having married her, against precise directives of government, yet he has shown me that he understands his error now and is repentant.

Moreover, he has intimated to me certain facts about this woman which would bear further scrutiny.

JUDGE. What facts are these?

STURMAN *looks to* ROBERT.

ROBERT. She has dismissed my son's nurse, a good Protestant woman, against my wishes.

She teaches him to speak the Irish tongue. I do not understand him and I would understand my son.

She has once or twice, in secret . . . she has attended Mass.

JUDGE. Mass? You are sure?

ROBERT. She waits for the darkness. She takes my son in one hand and a candle in the other. I have followed her.

She is acquainted with the desperate Tory, Pierce Kinsellagh.

JUDGE. These are serious accusations.

ROBERT. I do not accuse her, Sir. I only tell the truth. I think it is my duty to tell the truth to the Court.

JUDGE. And you were not aware of these traits before you made her your wife?

ROBERT. No, Sir. She was different then.

JUDGE. But you must have realised that by marrying an Irish girl you were . . .

ROBERT. I realised nothing.

JUDGE. Could it be that you cared not about these things until they proved a liability to your own well-being?

ROBERT. That is not true.

JUDGE. Your marrying with Irish could be seen as disaffection in itself.

ROBERT. I am a good English . . . . man.

I am a good Englishman.

I wish I had not married her. I wish I had not met her.

Pause.

STURMAN. It is true the woman is beguiling.

When she broke upon me at my desk she threatened me with witchcraft.

JUDGE. Do you cry witch?

STURMAN. I do not cry witch. If she is a witch then so is every native of this land. She is merely possessed of that evil, endemic in her breed, which moves beneath us even as we speak and won't be stayed by transplantation.

Let us know our business here.

Is it our business to move this man, a useful man, to the wastes of Connaught, exposing his son to the devil and his own? Or is it our business to cleanse this land?

I say, let this man remain on his estate and raise his son for Cromwell.

JUDGE. And his wife?

STURMAN. . . . Let the woman fall to me.

Scene Five

The bedroom of the Manor House.

MADELEINE *is sitting beside the cradle, reading to Ralph. There is the sound of voices and then SUSANEH enters and stops in the doorway.*

SUSANEH. Madeleine.

MADELEINE. What is it?

That's a terrible look, Susaneh.

SUSANEH. You must fly. Take Ralph and fly from here.
Troops are riding to arrest you. I cannot say how long you
have, perhaps but minutes now.

MADELEINE. We lost the appeal?

Where's Robert?

SUSANEH. Robert found words for himself.

MADELEINE. But not for me.

SUSANEH. I'm sorry. Things were said of you, dangerous
things. They mean to take Ralph and I would not see you
parted.

MADELEINE. What things?

SUSANEH. Come now. I have horses at the door.

MADELEINE. What things?

SUSANEH. That you go to Mass. That your friends are Tories.

It is Sturman who has done this. He can fashion truth the
way he will. He has your life.

MADELEINE. No one has my life. I have my life.

SUSANEH. Come then. We must go.

MADELEINE. It was Robert said those things?

SUSANEH. It was.

MADELEINE. They're true.

SUSANEH. I care not. Where is your cloak?

Madeleine.

MADELEINE. No. I will take nothing from this house.

SUSANEH. You need a cloak.

MADELEINE. I'll leave it all for burning.

SUSANEH. You shall have mine then.

MADELEINE. If he wants rid of me so much let him burn it all.

SUSANEH. Madeleine, please. Bring the child.

MADELEINE. You go now, Susaneh. I won't have you caught.

SUSANEH . I will see you safely on your way and do not, do not try to tell me no. I can match you, will for will.

Bring the child, and something warm to wrap him in.

MADELEINE (*standing over the cot*). Did Robert . . . does he know they would take him from me?

SUSANEH. Yes.

MADELEINE He knows?

SUSANEH. I see now how the world divides. There are those with goodness in their hearts and those without. That's all. You have a good heart, Madeleine. Solomon always said so. Come.

Scene Seven

The hallway of Rathconran House.

There is a heavy and continuous banging at the door.
SUSANEH appears in her night clothes and hurries to open it.
ROBERT bursts in.

ROBERT. Where is she?

Tell me where she is. She has my son.

SUSANEH. She is not here.

ROBERT. It was you. You warned her.

SUSANEH. Yes. Did you think I would close my eyes and hear her torn to pieces?

ROBERT. Where have you hidden her? Tell me.

I have men and I will see this place in flames unless you tell me where she is.

SUSANEH. I do not know. She would not endanger me with knowing, that's the kind of care she takes.

ROBERT. You should not have done this. This is bad Susaneh. Care? What do you know of her care? It is between myself and her.

SUSANEH. It is between us all.

Now leave this house. I will not see you more.

Get out.

ROBERT. I'll find her. Be sure of that. She has Ralph and cannot travel far. I will have her by the morning.

SUSANEH. How far will mother and child not go in search of safety?

ROBERT. I would not harm my son. Is that what she has told you? Do you think me monstrous?

SOLOMON *enters, also in his night clothes. He is very weak.*

SOLOMON. Robert? Can it be you who brings this clamour to my house?

Pause.

ROBERT. Solomon.

Forgive me.

(*Embracing him.*) Please forgive me.

ROBERT *goes.*

SOLOMON. Robert. Wait.

SUSANEH. Let him go. (*Shouting.*) I am ashamed to know him.

SOLOMON. Hush, woman. He is frightened. Don't you see?

SUSANEH. Then let him find his courage. Like the rest of us. Now do you see the way of him?

SOLOMON. I might be just the same if I had lost my wife and child.

SUSANEH. You would never give us cause to leave.

SOLOMON. I feel I should go after him.

SUSANEH. I feel you should come back to bed.

Solomon Winter, don't look at me like that.

He'll be back. He'll need you more than ever now.

SOLOMON. Do you think he'll find her?

SUSANEH. No.

SOLOMON. Poor creatures. It's a terrible world to be adrift in.

She goes to him and they hold each other.

Scene Eight

A Tory camp on the edge of the Wicklow hills.

It is dark. There is the occasional sound of movement and whispered words. MADELEINE *and* PIERCE *are side by side, staring into the night.*

MADELEINE. I took a room by the harbour. I could see the ship from the window. I passed the days on the quay, watching the deck. There wasn't a glimpse of her to be had. And then, one fresh morning, it sailed. I thought the sea would freeze, or split apart as it did for the Israelites. But the ship sailed on . . . .

PIERCE (*with barely controlled anger*). You should have come to me. Why did you listen to her?

MADELEINE. She was right. They would have had you in chains. I would have lost the both of you.

PIERCE. That's not yourself you're thinking of, is it?

MADELEINE. Perhaps it is.

PIERCE. You led her a merry dance, Maddy.

MADELEINE. I never meant to. You know that.

Pause.

Someone said they use the servants worse than any slave. A slave's for life and worth a little care, but a servant, who'll be gone in five years, seven . . .

PIERCE. They'll never tame Killaine. She'll be very small and let-alone by day, then send herself to the moon at night and step amongst the stars.

MADELEINE. She's stronger than she seems.

PIERCE. She is that.

MADELEINE. Do you think she's alive?

PIERCE. Do you?

MADELEINE. Yes.

PIERCE. Then so she is.

Pause.

MADELEINE. I wish I was looking from very far away. I used to have that, Pierce. Remember? It used to drive you to distraction.

PIERCE. You'll get it back.

Pause.

Are you cold?

I'm sleeping tonight. We can lie close together with the little lad between us. It's terrible rough, Maddy.

MADELEINE. For an English lady?

PIERCE. That's not what I meant.

MADELEINE. Isn't it?

PIERCE. I always wanted the best for you. I still do.

MADELEINE. Pierce . . .

PIERCE. It's all right. You don't have to say it. I'm not one for making the same mistake twice.

I'm just glad to have you in my gaze.

MADELEINE. Thank you.

PIERCE. But leave me my hopes, will you?

She smiles. He almost smiles.

We'll be moving on before dawn. Are you ready for travelling?

MADELEINE. Yes.

PIERCE (*seeing how depressed she is*). You'll reach the other side of it, Maddy.

MADELEINE. I am so afraid.

PIERCE. I won't be leaving you now.

MADELEINE. It's not that. It's not that. I don't know how to say it.

PIERCE. Are you telling me you're lost for words?

MADELEINE. Everything I thought I knew is gone.

Everything I held to. Can I have been so wrong?

PIERCE. I'll give you something to know then: know we must drive those people from our land. It's all you need. It's a pure thought. The strongest kind.

Look at everyone about you. Such different people we have been, such different lives but that is all we know and so we are the same now: back at the beginning. Back with the pack.

And so will you be, Maddy. You can't change your blood, or your eyes, or your heart. So will you be soon.

ACT FIVE

Scene One

In a clearing, in a wood.

It is a misty, howling evening. From one side of the clearing, a voice comes.

ROBERT. Madeleine Preston? Are you there?

From the other side, a voice answers.

MADELEINE. My name is Maddy O'Hart.

ROBERT. Are you alone and unarmed?

MADELEINE. I am.

Are you alone and unarmed?

ROBERT. I am.

Have you brought the child?

Pause.

Step out into the clearing and I will step out.

Slowly, through the mist, MADELEINE *and* ROBERT *emerge. They stop, several paces from each other.*

ROBERT. I knew you would not refuse me.

A soldier thought he saw you once. A woman and a child, swimming in the Slaney, laughing. She ran. Was it you?

I have searched, this last year, for sight or sound of you. You disappeared into the air. I questioned every man we took.

I offered a reward for Pierce Kinsellagh in the hope that he might lead me to you.

MADELEINE. We do not sell our own. You should know that by now.

The man who brought your message . . .

ROBERT. It won him his life.

MADELEINE. He said you work for Sturman.

ROBERT. I work for my country.

MADELEINE. I hope you are happy, Robert. I have tried to picture you happy.

Pause.

There is a sound from amongst the trees on ROBERT's *side of the clearing.*

ROBERT. Wolves.

Let me see Ralph now.

MADELEINE. Tell me of Solomon and Susaneh. I have looked for them many times amongst the people on the highway.

ROBERT. They do not go. Protestants are exempt now on payment of a fine. Madeleine . . .

MADELEINE. I am glad for them.

Tell them . . . Please tell them I will never forget their kindness.

ROBERT. Madeleine, let Ralph come forward now.

I have longed to see him. You cannot know how much.

Let him come here to me. I have presents for his birthday.

MADELEINE. Ralph is dead.

He died five weeks ago.

ROBERT. Dead?

It is his birthday.

MADELEINE. He is dead.

He came and saw the way things are and went away again.

ROBERT. No. You are lying.

MADELEINE. I have learnt to lie, Robert, but I would not lie with this. I do not want to hurt you. I only came to tell you he is dead. All the people that knew and it was only you I wanted.

ROBERT. This is evil. In truth. He has been asking for me, hasn't he? You think I will go away and leave him alone.

MADELEINE. No.

ROBERT. You think to keep him from me.

(*Calling.*) Ralph.

Ralph, it is your father. Come to me, Ralph.

MADELEINE. Why do you think I came here? I came because I knew you would not believe me and I wanted you to see it in my eyes. Look at my eyes, Robert. He is dead. It is over.

Pause.

We did some fine destructive work between us.

ROBERT. You killed him. If you had not taken him from me . . . if you had not taken him he would not have . . .

MADELEINE. And why did I take him? Tell me the choice. No. No, this isn't it.

ROBERT. What then? You're doing this . . . You're the one who comes here saying he is . . .

MADELEINE. Blame me if you will. But it's the truth.

She moves her hand.

ROBERT. Don't move. I'm warning you.

She slowly pulls a toy from her cloak, the same one she used to frighten STURMAN, *and holds it out to him.*

He does not move. She throws it gently across to him.

MADELEINE. You chose it for him. It was his favourite. He would want for you to have it.

ROBERT *looks at it, then crouches and picks it up.*

MADELEINE. He was strong and happy while we lived in the woods. But soldiers came to fell the trees, forced us back to lower ground. There was fever there. He cried a lot and died.

ROBERT. Oh my God, he is dead.

He begins to sob silently.

What have I lost? What have I lost?

MADELEINE. Robert?

We are finished now. There is nothing left between us.

Perhaps that is good. I have even found a sort of peace. Everything is very simple. I hope you find it too.

ROBERT. You bitch.

MADELEINE. What?

ROBERT. You Irish bitch. If only I had known that's what it takes to make you happy, to watch your child die, to whore it with barbarians, to kill and terrorise and . . .

MADELEINE. You're wrong.

ROBERT. I'm glad I kill you. I'm glad I kill you all. All of you.

There is shame behind his eyes.

MADELEINE. Nothing you can say will touch me.

I do what I do because I have to and because I hope that one day, the people who come after me will have their lives for themselves without this pulling back and pulling back. That they will have their lives to fly like falcons, off their hands and back again as they will. It is a dream. And I will not give it up.

The only thing I can't forgive you for, the only thing, is that you would not see the strength you had beside you, right beside you. And you would not hold me by the hand and walk forward with me to take our lives.

I loved you, and would have loved you always. Always.

Maybe that was not enough.

She takes out a piece of paper and holds it out.

It is a map that shows his grave. You will want to go and see him.

He walks towards her and takes it. They look into each other's eyes. She reaches out and touches his face. He lets her.

Pause.

MADELEINE. What happens now, Robert?

I turn around to walk and find a bullet in my back?

ROBERT. What do you mean?

MADELEINE. I have lived beneath the sky a while now and it has taught me many things. Almost as canny as Killaine, I am. And I have learnt the difference between the sound of wolves and the sound of men with guns.

You are not alone. You have your people with you.

ROBERT. Yes.

MADELEINE. And I have mine.

The lights dim. There is the sound of a hundred guns being cocked. The lights are gone.

The End

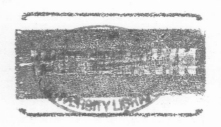